# COUNSELORS,
# COMFORTERS,
# AND FRIENDS

# COUNSELORS, COMFORTERS, AND FRIENDS

## SHELLEY CHAPIN

VICTOR BOOKS®

A DIVISION OF SCRIPTURE PRESS PUBLICATIONS INC.
USA CANADA ENGLAND

Copyediting: Jerry Yamamoto, Barbara Williams
Cover Design: Joe DeLeon
Cover Illustration: Ted Wright

---

### Library of Congress Cataloging-in-Publication Data

Chapin, Shelley.
    Counselors, comforters, and friends / Shelley Chapin.
      p.   cm. — (Equipped for ministry series)
    Includes bibliographical references.
    ISBN 0-89693-910-3
    1. Consolation.   2. Suffering—Religious aspects—Christianity.
    3. Grief—Religious aspects—Christianity.     I. Title.  II. Series.
    BV4905.2.C43   1992
    259'.6—dc20                              91-42033
                                                       CIP

---

   2   3   4   5   6   7   8   9  10   Printing/Year  96  95  94  93

# CONTENTS

# PREFACE

## A Letter to the Church

There is little need to argue with the facts: People all over the world are suffering many griefs, losses, fears, deaths, and unfulfilled needs. More than ever before, the church is finding herself in the position of counselor, supporter, comforter, adviser, protector, and friend. The needs are great among God's people and within the community at large. People are looking for comfort, and they are looking to the church—to you and to me—to provide a cup of cool water.

I know that even broaching this subject makes most of us "in the ministry" cringe! There are infinitely more needs than a pastor and staff can adequately meet. And the hunger for comfort falls in so many different categories: alcoholism and drug dependencies, all manners of physical and familial abuse, eating disorders, divorce, addictions, psychological problems, financial strains and stress. The list seems endless!

How can one minister possibly address all these needs within the church? The answer is simple; it cannot be done—not by one or two or even a staff of twenty. People are hurting, and we cannot silence their cries.

There is a valid argument on the ministerial front concerning this matter. Faced with the variety of needs that do exist, one pastor of a large church recently stated the argument rather concisely. Since the church does not provide legal assistance for her members, why should she provide counseling support? Why, indeed?

The dilemma is not an easy one, and I can readily sympathize with the pastor whose duties alone require far more time than can possibly be squeezed from the hourglass. We can try to ignore the problems as if they don't exist. We can send our people elsewhere for the help they need. We can try to spiritualize the problems and hope our people resolve their own sufferings and sins. Or we can open wide our doors, prepare our staff and our people, roll up our sleeves, and "dive into" the experiences of life. After all, where can a person turn, if not to those who are most deeply acquainted with comfort?

This book will not attempt an exhaustive look at all of the needs we have mentioned so far. There is no way to do justice to the issues in such a short space. I have chosen, instead, one facet of our need—the need for comfort in our various griefs, compassion in our moments of need.

The church is filled with those who are grieving. Physical illness or death, chronic emotional or physical pain, relational griefs, depression—this book will address the need for comfort and the ability of the church to offer that blessed comfort to those who are suffering. God's people need a brush with love.

I have a personal interest in this matter. A cancer patient myself, I have experienced, firsthand, the fears, the pains, and the needs that arise from such suffering. And I have experienced the longing for someone somewhere who can offer true comfort. Such a gift is rare.

The pain of grief runs deep. When we are confronted with grief, our need for comfort encompasses the physical, the mental, the emotional, and the spiritual. We need the breadth of God's love, one day at a time. We need a new perspective, a listening ear, an awareness of purpose, the chance to discover God all over again.

The idea for this book was born some years ago. After starting my journey with cancer in October of 1982, I began to travel and speak to churches, hospitals, medical schools, and conferences, telling all who would listen about the lessons I had learned in the company of suffering.

I found myself, on many occasions, going with a pastor to the hospital or to the homes of those who were struggling. The time was always precious to me. I discovered a connection between myself and the sufferers that I had never understood before. God was working in personal, internal ways. He was alive! And He was granting me the privilege of sharing in some of the most important moments of a person's life.

During those times of visitation, I was also keenly aware of the frustrations and limitations felt by the minister. Each week there were new people to visit, new sufferings to share, new hurts to soothe, and no time to follow through on last week's list. It dawned on me that people are suffering in silence, and the church is missing a real opportunity for ministry and growth.

What happens after I board the plane for a church in another city? What happens to the needy on this week's list when others step in to take their places? What happens to the minister who gives more time away than that which exists on the hands of the clock?

What normally happens is this: The pastoral staff (sometimes one member!) does all that is within the realm of possibility to visit, to pray, to offer concern, to stay abreast of the urgent — all the while carrying out the "normal" duties of running a church! Unfortunately, in the wake of the urgent, many are the people who fall "between the cracks" in need of some lasting support. Our ministers need our help; the church needs our willingness to be involved.

What I am simply saying is that no one pastor or pastoral staff can meet all of the needs alone, and no one pastor or staff needs to try. We can work together as a body to help one another. We can pool our gifts and our resources to minister to those within our midst. When we work together, the result is more than satisfying, it is life-transforming.

Every church is equipped with those who are merciful — those whose hearts are ripe for investing time and love in the lives of those who are grieving. People do want to help; and willing hearts, mixed with some good organization and wise training, can make a huge difference in the lives of those who need comfort.

This book deals specifically with establishing an ongoing program within the local church for ministering to those who are suffering or who have suffered a loss. What I have attempted to do is provide an organized, clear, understandable way of establishing and maintaining such a ministry, staffed by those who are gifted, capable, and willing to fulfill this very important need.

The body of believers within each local church contains a myriad of gifted people who will, themselves, feel far more useful and fulfilled if given the opportunity to discover and exercise their gifts. We need to train and use our most valuable resources.

While I know I am addressing only one of the areas of need in our world today, it is my prayer that, once the church sees such a ministry take hold, the same principles can be put to work in the other areas of need. The working together of the body of Christ is nothing short of a deeply satisfying experience for all.

This book is dedicated to those with the gifts of mercy and love, and to all ministers everywhere who are faced with the difficult yet privileged task of ministering to those who grieve. Allow me the joy of sharing with you an awareness, a perspective, and a plan for ministering to those who need comfort in your midst.

We do have the resources: loving arms, open hearts, eternal perspectives, and the comfort of our very wise and compassionate Lord.

# SECTION ONE:
## Exploring the Need for Comfort

We put no stumbling block in anyone's path, so that our ministry will not be discredited. Rather, as servants of God we commend ourselves in every way: in great endurance; in troubles, hardships, and distresses; in beatings, imprisonments and riots; in hard work, sleepless nights and hunger; in purity, understanding, patience and kindness; in the Holy Spirit and in sincere love; in truthful speech and in the power of God; with weapons of righteousness in the right hand and in the left; through glory and dishonor, bad report and good report; genuine, yet regarded as impostors; known, yet regarded as unknown; dying, and yet we live on; beaten, and yet not killed; sorrowful, yet always rejoicing; poor, yet making many rich; having nothing, and yet possessing everything. We have spoken freely to you, Corinthians, and opened wide our hearts to you. We are not withholding our affection from you, but you are withholding yours from us. As a fair exchange—I speak as to my children—open wide your hearts also.

2 Corinthians 6:3-13

# ONE

## The Reality of Suffering, Grief, and Death

We rarely think of the Apostle Paul as a sufferer, but we can see from his "list" in 2 Corinthians that he was well acquainted with pain. He experienced grief and death in a variety of emotional, physical, and mental ways, and yet he knew joy. He came into his faith expecting to honor and serve his Lord, and Paul was not disappointed.

Pain, death, and the process of grieving are not strangers to the Christian. Since the beginning of time as we know it, believers and nonbelievers alike have come face-to-face with suffering and death. Difficulties are part of life; they are not erased with conversion and commitment.

The first step in developing a ministry of compassion and comfort in the church lies in admitting the need for such a ministry. As long as we continue to "dress" our needs the way we "dress" our bodies, pretending not to have any hurt, we pass by one of the most sacred gifts we have in this world—the privilege of needing God and one another, of giving and receiving comfort.

Suffering is not something we must hide or a condition for which we must feel ashamed. Pain is part of our life experience on this earth; it is to be expected, not despised.

Jesus prepared His disciples for the trouble and grief they would face upon His departure. Paul reached out to nurture his brothers in their sufferings. Peter and James encouraged their readers to hold on in the midst of difficulty. In fact, if we see our losses from God's perspective, the very things we fear seem to bring growth.

I must admit that I was unable to see any good at the beginning of my own loss. When first confronted with cancer and a prognosis of a short time to live, all I could think was: "This has to be a mistake. God would never allow this to happen to me. After all, I'm serving Him." And I was not alone in my inability to grasp God's purpose.

I found that most of my Christian friends could accept the kind of persecution that comes from Christian service, but they were unable to accept the persecution of an illness. In many people's minds (and words!), there was a clear reluctance to view the cancer as something God was allowing and using in my life. It was much more comfortable for them to see the illness as an error of some kind. I still see skepticism and fear in some people's eyes as I relate both my pains and my joys.

We seem surprised that these bodies are earthly and that this earth is embroiled in the battle with sin. As Christians, we are neither removed from life here, nor are we removed from the painful trials that surround us—trials that include physical illnesses and limitations. What people need in the midst of their various sufferings is a place where they can go to find truth and comfort. They do not need a place where suffering and death are denied.

It seems interesting to me that social organizations, such as Hospice, the Ronald McDonald house, support groups, and shelters of various kinds, readily acknowledge the obvious and the needs that go along with the sufferings. The church, however, seems slow to both admit the problems and minister to the people. We are almost ashamed to suffer and seek comfort. Somehow, the facing of our pain and the admission of our needs has come to symbolize weakness and lack of faith.

My own opinion is that this attitude is merely a result of fear. If we insist that painful things can't happen to the Christian, maybe they won't! (We call this "positive thinking.") Such reasoning sounds like the very tactic I once used to convince myself that monsters didn't really live under my bed.

I had a ritual I followed each evening. In order to ensure my safety through the night, I looked under the bed right before jumping in for the duration. In my game, such a precaution rendered the monsters incapable of entering their hiding place, and I could sleep securely. Sound familiar? As simplistic as it may seem, we apply a bit of that same logic to the pains that threaten our comforts and plans.

We have developed a theology of suffering that places the possibility of pain outside of the experience of the "good Christian," particularly during our prime years. We live as if God owes us certain happinesses and comforts, and we have no room for sufferings' gifts.

The tragedy of such a perspective is that we miss so much when we are unwilling to look at the reality of grief and loss. The sufferings and deaths we experience in this world teach us more than we know. God promises to work everything together for good, and that promise includes the painful.

The most important step we can take, as a church, is to remove the stigmas of needing and reaching out for help. If we see suffering, in its variety of forms, as a reality rather than a failure, we can begin to reach out to those in need. Scripture teaches us that some of the deepest lessons of faith are companions to pain. May we join together to make those lessons known.

### "Unspeakable Things"

There are few believers who have never heard of Job's suffering. In fact, Job's life alone readily refutes those who suggest that grief comes only to the disobedient sinner. God said there was no one on earth like Job (Job 1:8), and yet He allowed the unspeakable to occur in the life of His beloved servant.

The unspeakable is the very thing that frightens us, just as it frightened Job (3:25). God's servant went from being a well-respected, successful man to feeling as if his life had no meaning—past, present, or future. Job hadn't prepared himself to be a sufferer; it was a role he had never been taught to play.

The Book of Job is an insightful, personal account of a man in the midst of grief. We see Job's progression through disbelief, worship, weeping, despair, weariness, searching, loneliness, anger, and back again. We see him lose wealth, family, friends, respect, and purpose. We see him feel isolated, betrayed, and helplessly afraid. Job was allowed, by God, to experience some of the most extreme losses a person can ever experience.

The end of the story, however, is not one of despair and hopelessness. The end of the story is one of growth, life, faith, and trust. In the midst of his ongoing pain, with no end to suffering promised or in sight, we see Job come to the place where he can say, "My ears had heard of You, but now my eyes have seen You" (42:5). Job grew to see God through the very pain he feared.

### "Now My Eyes Have Seen You"

Doesn't it seem that Job's story is a mirror of our lives? I think so. Though few of us have tasted the degree of Job's sufferings, each of us has experienced the feelings that Job knew so well in his sorrow. We have all been touched by pain, yet few of us stop to observe our transformation in the midst of our loss.

When faced with suffering, most of us muster all of our courage and resources to remove the painful trial. While I am not suggesting that it is wrong to try and alter or better our circumstances, I am suggesting that we generally try all that is within our reach before considering the fact that God just might have something in mind for us through that pain.

Growth and truths that we've never known become our companions in grief, just as they became Job's. We simply must stop long enough to notice God's handiwork. Perhaps a few examples of this perspective will help.

### "Faith, Purer Than Gold"

> In this (our new life in Christ) you greatly rejoice, though now for a little while you may have had to suffer grief in all kinds of trials. These have come so that your faith—of greater worth than gold, which perishes even though refined by fire—may be proved genuine and may result in praise, glory, and honor when Jesus Christ is revealed (1 Peter 1:6-7).

Peter was preparing his readers for the various persecutions that would soon be a part of their "normal" Christian existence. Notice that the discipler neither promised an end to the sufferings nor suggested that the trials would come only to those who were leading sinful lives. Peter was addressing God's elect, strangers in the world, who have been chosen by God (vv. 1-2).

Peter knew that the suffering was real, and that it would likely continue. He wrote of purpose and perspective, not prevention. The eternal view of God promised both a reason and a reward: faith purified by pain and presented to God as a gift. Such purpose makes the suffering well worth the struggle.

### "Count It All Joy"

James also spoke of the various trials awaiting the believer. He too wrote of perspective, not cure. And the result of suffering in the eyes of James? Joy. Pure joy.

> Consider it pure joy, my brothers, whenever you face trials of many kinds, because you know that the testing of your faith develops perseverance. Perseverance must finish its work so that you may be mature and complete, not lacking anything (James 1:2-4).

Can purity and completion really be the result of wading through a variety of trials? Apparently so. We well understand this concept in the parenting role.

If your first-grader comes home after school one day and remarks that she's not planning to attend anymore, what do you say? Or suppose your middle school student decides that homework just isn't his "thing." He'd rather play with his friends. Is that acceptable behavior?

Why do we urge our children to make good choices? Why do we work so hard to train them in righteousness, to develop their talents and gifts? Do we present them with only those options that they will find enjoyable? Or do we expect them to experience and grow from discomfort?

A concerned, dedicated parent hungers for the child to become mature and complete. If parenting were only caretaking for a few years, we would never go to all the trouble to correct and train. But we want more for our children than momentary comfort. We want maturity.

How much more does God long to train us for maturity? And how better to teach us than through those experiences that bring us face-to-face with trust, humility, and dependence on Him?

God knows that the muscles of our maturity would never develop if it weren't for trials of various kinds. We are naturally lazy and comfort-seeking people. We do not pursue spiritual maturity, because it hurts.

The growing of our faith requires that we lay aside the old and make way for the new, day after day and experience after experience. Maturity requires that we allow God to grow us up—a longing that meets discomfort and results in joy. James perceived the final gain, and that gain makes the cost worthwhile.

### "An Unworthy World"
If suffering is difficult to accept, so is physical death. Even Jesus' followers thought Him capable of fixing just about any problem ...as long as the person hadn't died.

We struggle with dying physically, and we struggle with dying to self. After all, dying to self requires that we trust God with our most intimately important possession—our very own beings.

When I first struggled with the thought of being "terminal," I felt so helpless to correct the problem. I was raised to be an "endurer" and to find solutions. Suddenly, the solutions were eternal, and they were in God's hand.

After several months of struggling, I began to see that physical death was only an image of my real problem. I had never before been placed in such a position of dependency on God. I needed His support, strength, courage, and sight. I was afraid of my own limitations. I needed to learn to die to "myself." And as I began to learn that lesson, I began to taste freedom.

We enjoy reading the first part of the eleventh chapter of Hebrews. The story is one of faith and accomplishment, glory and honor. Yet we seem to stop short of the complete account. While many were able to perform wonders in this world, others were specially chosen for wonders in the next.

> Others were tortured and refused to be released, so that they might gain a better resurrection. Some faced jeers and flogging, while still others were chained and put in prison. They were stoned; they were sawed in two; they were put to death by the sword. They went about in sheepskins and goatskins,

18

> destitute, persecuted, and mistreated—the world was
> not worthy of them (Heb. 11:35-38).

Though this is a painful description, it also reveals an important truth. All of us physically die, and we all must come to the place where we put ourselves completely in God's care. We know this is true, but we don't accept death very well. We hold onto this world and our own abilities tightly, and we act as if death is our greatest enemy.

Sometimes the end result of suffering is more suffering. Sometimes the end result of faithful prayer is the death of a loved one. Sometimes dying to self means that we release something very precious to us. Common to all these scenarios is our need to trust God in the midst of the storm.

In a way, we think we can trick God. If we pray, if we behave, if we do the right things the right way, then God will reward us by taking away the hurt. That is not the way the game of Christian obedience is played.

God asks simply that we "trust and obey," and that we believe He withholds no good thing from those He loves. When we try to orchestrate our own reward, we undermine the real one.

We die to live, and in death our life has its true significance. Paul stated the dilemma clearly when he wrote:

> For to me, to live is Christ and to die is gain. If I am
> to go on living in the body, this will mean fruitful
> labor for me. Yet what shall I choose? I do not know!
> I am torn between the two: I desire to depart and be
> with Christ, which is better by far; but it is more neces-
> sary for you that I remain in the body (Phil. 1:21-24).

For Paul, death is the final passage from this life to true life. He welcomed physical death because he had learned how to die to himself. Think about it. Long before his life was in danger, Paul had settled the score with God.

> I consider everything a loss compared to the surpass-
> ing greatness of knowing Christ Jesus my Lord, for
> whose sake I have lost all things. I consider them
> rubbish, that I may gain Christ (Phil. 3:8).

Dying to ourselves (to our way of doing things) makes the path straight. We see far more clearly when we allow God to lead the way. One day at a time is sufficient, and death means life, not a dreadful end.

The church needs to examine her fear of death. Instead of avoiding the concept, we need to teach our people the reality of death and the hope involved in trusting God. "The man who loves his life will lose it," Jesus said, "while the man who hates his life in this world will keep it for eternal life" (John 12:25). Such is the perspective we need to grasp and convey.

People will always fear the process of dying, but we need not fear the transformation of death. If we grow accustomed to death's role, then we will better know how to play our own scene as it is required.

### "The Real Need"
I have chosen only a few examples from the wealth of God's Word. We could literally write a volume on God's sufferers alone. In that volume, what we would see is more of the faith we've seen in the passages discussed. As painful as suffering and death may be, the end result for the child of God is good. We need not perpetuate the rumor that God sees no value in our struggles.

There is a real need for comfort in our churches, and the meeting of that need begins with the admission of the need. Suffering, death, and grief are all very real; they are not the exception to the rule.

How we, as ministers and lay leaders, see suffering directly affects the kind of comfort we offer. I pray we will see through God's perspective and not through the limited vision that is man's.

Pain and loss are neither mistakes nor judgments in and of themselves, nor are they negative happenings. They are realities, and they are intricately woven into God's design for you and for me.

# TWO

## The Basic Needs of Those Who Suffer

Suffering people often feel like strangers in an otherwise "normal" world. They feel alone and lonely, misunderstood yet desirous of understanding. They go about the business of life, but there is little of the energy that once seemed plentiful.

Sufferers don't know why they feel so weary, nor do they comprehend why others can't see their pain. They are in need of comfort and compassion, a listening ear and a warm touch.

### Back to the Basics

When a young baby cries, the parent runs through a mental checklist of the basics. Is he hungry? Is she wet? Is she sick? Is something hurting him? Once the checklist is complete, then all that remains is the gentle touch that only a parent can offer.

Suffering brings us "back to the basics." No longer do the myriad of life's demands play an important role. Instead, all that remains are the essentials of relationship. We long to be loved and to have the chance to love, to be heard and to have the chance to hear, to be viewed through eyes of compassion and to have the chance to see.

Paul was no stranger to suffering, yet he did not hide his hurts, his fears, or his needs. He used his letters to the churches to speak openly of his own life and to ask for their compassion and understanding.

When we examine the contents of Paul's requests, we find that they were really quite simple. Paul requested prayer and the company of the people he loved. He requested kindness and understanding. Paul requested love, obedience, and the "carrying on" of the work he had begun.

While a variety of needs exist for the sufferer, I have chosen three general needs that I feel encompass most of the other needs we experience: the need for the people we love, the need for acceptance, and the need for perspective. Perhaps these can serve as the framework for the ministry of comfort in the church.

## The Need for Those We Love

The main need of the sufferer is the company of family and friends. While time alone is also necessary, those who suffer are quickly reminded of the importance of relationships. Sometimes those who have been the busiest have the greatest desire for the presence of loved ones. Suffering puts our priorities in place and provides us with the opportunity to reevaluate our needs.

Paul hungered for the presence of his disciples as he faced his pains. There was no greater gift the churches could send him than Timothy, Epaphroditus, Tychicus, or Onesimus (Phil. 2:19-30; Eph. 6:21-22; Col. 4:7-9). And Paul's love for Timothy was as a father to his son—a love that greatly enabled Paul to serve the Lord faithfully.

Jesus also sought the comfort of His friends. When making final preparations for His death, Jesus' only request was the presence of Peter, James, and John.

> He began to be sorrowful and troubled. Then He said to them, "My soul is overwhelmed with sorrow to the point of death. Stay here and keep watch with Me" (Matt. 26:37-38).

There was nothing the disciples could do to remove Jesus' suffering, but their company was enough to offer Him comfort. Sadly, they did not understand the need and slept instead of sharing His grief, but His longing remained the same. He desired the company of His beloved companions.

Elijah too knew despair, and that despair was directly related to his aloneness. He soared to heights of spiritual satisfaction as he watched God deliver fire from heaven, but faced with the threats of Jezebel, the prophet grew weary. He felt alone. Hundreds of prophets had already been killed, and he was tired of the battle (1 Kings 19).

Before Jacob died, God provided a reunion with his son, Joseph. For years, Jacob had been depressed over what he believed to be the death of his favorite son. Jacob's loss was real, and God well understood the pain. While Jacob could yet rejoice, God reunited him with his son and gave him days filled with the comfort of Joseph's presence (Gen. 37–50).

All through Scripture, we see pictures of relationships: friendships that are more important than activities, burdens that are shared. People are important to us in our suffering. We need not be afraid of bothering someone or becoming a burden. The church is a haven, where the love of God is known and the needs of His children can be lifted and shared. Offering the gift of comfort to those who hurt is a tremendous blessing.

### The Need for Acceptance

When someone we love is suffering, we generally attempt to fix the problem. Though well-intentioned, our attempts can quickly move us off the track of what the sufferer really needs.

There are times when fixing is appropriate and much desired. There are other times, however, when we cannot fix, and when fixing is not at all what the sufferer wants or really needs.

I smile whenever I read about Peter's feeble promise to protect Jesus from harm. It reminds me of the old cartoon where the woman is tied to the railroad track, and at the last possible moment Dudley Do-Right steps in with, "I'll save you!"

Peter longed to "save" Jesus from the very task He came to perform. It was a well-intentioned gesture, but one that missed the whole point of the sacrifice. Jesus didn't need Peter to fix the situation; He needed Peter to accept the situation and walk with Him through the trial (Matt. 16:21-23).

We have come to equate acceptance with resignation, and the two are not compatible. When I suggest that we accept a person's circumstances, I am not suggesting that we "give up" or "resign" ourselves to the problem. What I am simply saying is this: Acceptance is a much needed gift we can extend to the sufferer. It is a place to "begin."

I once knew a young woman who was struggling deeply with

the way her life had turned out. Since she was beautiful and had been quite popular in high school, she dreamed great dreams for her future.

At the young age of seventeen, her plans drastically changed. In a moment of adolescent passion, she became pregnant and quickly assumed adult responsibilities. By the time her mid-twenties had rolled around, she awoke to a life that had no correlation to her dreams.

I still remember her words: "I can't do this anymore." Yet every time she said, "I can't," her family said, "You can," until it was too late. Taking her own life, she proved to everyone who knew her that she was unwilling to take the next step of life.

What happened? Where did her family and friends go wrong? What had they missed in her cries for help?

Like all of us, that young girl's family and friends wanted the best for her. They couldn't accept her depression because that presented a problem they couldn't solve. Instead of accepting the reality of her need, they kept pushing her to just get on with life and ignore the pain. She chose another route.

No one forced this young woman to take her own life. It was no one's fault but her own. Still, her loved ones missed an opportunity to reach out to her in her need. She wanted them to listen to her cries and take them seriously; she wanted them to accept her limitations.

I counsel hundreds of families who face illnesses or other losses. More times than not, the advice of the family members to the sufferer is, "You need to fight," or, "Don't talk that way," or, "We're going to beat this thing."

Again, it is not that fighting is wrong, it is just that it is out of proportion to the real pain and needs of the sufferer. When a person is struggling, the experience embedded in the pain is just as important as the cure, if not more so. When we don't allow the person to talk about the struggle or feel the emotions that accompany the pain, we become stumbling blocks in the process of healing.

If Job's friends had only stopped at their initial response. What they did for Job in the beginning days of his loss was exactly what he needed from them. They sat with him in the ashes, and they wept. They accepted their friend's situation, and in doing so gave comfort (Job 2:11-13).

24

The problem came when Job started speaking. Depressed because of his losses, he shared his feelings. That's when the advice broke loose.

Job ventured to share his grief, only to find that his grief was unacceptable in the spiritual economy of his friends. The loneliness grew in proportion to their inability to relate to his suffering.

The object of offering comfort is providing a place in which the sufferer can find rest, acceptance, and a listening ear. Sadly, Job's friends had no such place to offer. But this doesn't have to happen in the church.

Think of the hundreds of people who came in touch with Jesus during His earthly ministry. Whether willing or unwilling to receive truth, whether acting responsibly or irresponsibly, whether happy, sad, depressed, or angry, Jesus accepted the person behind the pain. He knew the heart, and He looked past the situation to what was really going on inside.

Accepting someone's situation is not condoning their behavior or resigning them to a fate of grief. Accepting someone's situation is merely that—observing, listening, sharing, and "being there." Acceptance is the beginning of healing.

What we hide becomes tomorrow's pain. What we share and accept becomes a stepping stone to tomorrow's growth.

## The Need for Perspective

The sufferer often feels lost in the midst of a world that once made sense. When we are hurting in some way, it is easy to lose our perspective. What we once knew seems muddled; what we once planned seems impossible. We need perspective in order to "see" the value in pain.

When God finally spoke to Job, He brought Job's suffering into perspective (Job 38–41). In fact, it has always amused me that God did not mention Job's suffering. Instead, He turned Job's eyes off of himself and onto the faithfulness of God. The strategy worked!

> Where were you when I laid the earth's foundation?
> Tell me, if you understand. . . . Who shut up the sea
> behind doors when it burst forth from the womb,
> when I made the clouds its garment and wrapped it in

25

> thick darkness, when I fixed limits for it and set its
> doors and bars in place, when I said, "This far you
> may come and no farther; here is where your proud
> waves halt"? (Job 38:4, 8-11)

God didn't mention Job's pain because it was obvious, from His descriptions, that He *knows* and *controls* everything. Job was safely nestled in God's care, and such a realization brought perspective to Job for the first time.

Joseph seemed to grasp the importance of perspective too. Perhaps the long nights spent in prison or the hours he lay waiting for God to act taught him this important lesson.

I cannot know how he discovered God's sovereignty, but I do know that Joseph's timely reunion with his brothers reflected the kind of perspective that is known by few. Reunited with the brothers who betrayed him, he had the wisdom to share these words:

> Do not be distressed and do not be angry with your-
> selves for selling me here, because it was to save lives
> that God sent me ahead of you . . . God sent me
> ahead of you to preserve for you a remnant on earth
> and to save your lives by a great deliverance (Gen.
> 45:5, 7).

How did Joseph recognize such truth? How did he grasp God's purpose in his pain? Joseph had learned perspective, and such knowledge gave him the courage he needed to live one day at a time, obeying a God he trusted with his very life.

When we are grieving, we tend to feel as if nothing makes sense. It is difficult to remember the good days, and even more difficult to imagine life with meaning once again. Job struggled deeply with perspective. (See Job 3, 6, and 10 for insight.) Extending the gift of perspective to the sufferer is a much need-ed blessing.

We don't need to give easy answers or short verses from Scripture designed to explain away the pain. We don't need to offer "shoulds" and "shouldn'ts" or simple solutions. What we need to offer is a look at the bigger picture of purpose and meaning.

Be with the sufferer, accept the reality of the pain, and help the one who grieves see the larger scope of God's working in our lives. If the church can unite to offer such care, then those who hurt will find comfort and strength in the midst of the trial.

# THREE

## The Need for Comfort
## within the Church

I'll never forget my first exposure to public service. It was during my junior year in high school. We were required to volunteer at an organization of our choosing for eight Saturday mornings. Since I had always been interested in children, I chose an organization in Dallas called Children's Medical Center. Before I knew it, Saturday morning had rolled around, and I was off to the hospital for my first day as a young volunteer.

The physicians and nurses were great. They showed me around the wards, pointing out children who could use a little attention and rooms where I could take them to read or play. I quickly grew confident, and I had such a good experience the first day that I pledged my involvement for years.

The weeks went on. As I became a part of the lives of the children, I realized how much bigger the world is than I had thought. Up to that point, I had only known people "like me." My life had been sandwiched between fun and a few disappointments here and there. Yet at the hospital I found people with chronic pain and real loss—people whose lives and hearts were punctured by suffering.

My stint as a volunteer lasted years instead of weeks. Rather than "depressing" me, my service there opened my eyes to loving people in a deeper way. So significant was the impact that I have since continued my involvement with social services and nonprofit organizations, seeking to enrich my life by offering comfort to those in need. My own purpose has been fed by the hundreds of families whose smiles and tears left their mark on my heart.

## Letting Others Do the Work

If we counted the number of service organizations at work in the world, we would be counting for a very long time: the Peace Corps, the International Red Cross, United Way, Hospices, hospitals, mental health facilities, Alcoholics Anonymous, adoption agencies, Ronald McDonald houses, homes for unwed mothers, and a myriad of organizations designed to offer help to people of all ages and cultures who have some sort of need. And these organizations do an excellent job.

Think about the people you alone have known during a time of need. You've probably watched as a friend entered the hospital or died from an illness. You've probably known someone who received a much-wanted or long-awaited baby into the home.

You've seen vast numbers of homeless receive food and shelter from various groups who care. And you might have volunteered a day or two at a local food bank, suicide prevention center, or emergency shelter for battered women and children.

You might have called the local Hospice office for a family member who was dying. You might have received help from the Red Cross as the victim of a fire or flood. You might have given birth to a child through the gracious help of a home for unwed mothers. You might even have entered a shelter or sought food and clothing for your family when times were difficult. One way or another, we are all recipients of concern from social organizations.

What would our world be like without those organizations? Where would we be without people who believe in a cause and follow that belief through to hands-on involvement? Where would we be if the people weren't there to reach out when someone is in trouble?

Most of us are grateful that such caring places and people exist. In fact, most of us support at least one of those caring places or people. Telethons, mail appeals, personal visits, direction of the Spirit—all make us aware of what we can do to minister to people in need.

Where does the church fit into the picture? Does the church need to be involved? With so many good organizations and trained people "out there" ready to help, what can the church possibly add? After all, aren't we in danger of flooding the market or giving someone help that they might receive someplace else?

## Rolling Up Our Heartsleeves

Though this illustration is a bit "dramatic," allow me a moment of drama to make a point.

Imagine yourself a parent (which might not be too difficult for many of you!) with a young son who has just lost his girlfriend to the captain of the football team. Sound a bit familiar? Your child comes home from school and closes the door in such a way that you immediately recognize as trouble. He begins to climb the stairs as you approach, and you hear the barely audible but familiar voice utter, "Hullo."

As a parent, it is unthinkable to have this conversation:

"Hi, son. You look a bit down. Anything wrong?"

"Yeah. JoAnn broke up with me today. She's dating Rob now. What am I gonna do?"

"Son! Here's the number for the crisis hotline. They're professionals, you know. They'll be glad to help. Let me get you the phone!"

Just for a moment, allow yourself to imagine such a scenario. Couldn't a trained counselor help your son better than you? After all, a professional has heard these stories time and again. But, could a hotline operator give him love the way you can? What is the purpose of parental comforting?

Every parent is in the parenting game for a lifetime. To this day, I turn to my parents for their love and support, and I can't imagine that changing. When parents bring their first child home, they roll up their heartsleeves and go to work, committing themselves to love for the duration.

The church is family. I will grant you that there are a number of churches who haven't discovered the joy of living like a family, but that doesn't change the nature of God's design. He's designed the church to be the family of believers—brothers and sisters who care deeply for one another and whose love no social organization can duplicate.

Am I suggesting that the social organizations are worthless? Absolutely not! I would hate to imagine our world without those caring people. The church definitely needs the help of those who are "in the business." No one church group can possibly offer the variety of help that those in the congregation and the community might need.

The church does need to be involved, however. The pain is more severe when we have to pretend it doesn't exist or act as if we have our lives "together." Simply being able to share our hurts goes a long way in the healing process.

We need an environment in which it is permissible to need help and fashionable to reach out. A hurting member of a family needs the other members of the family to care—to roll up the heartsleeves and get to work.

## With Hearts Opened Wide

Paul wrote the Second Letter to the Corinthians as a letter from his heart. He had been resoundingly instructive with them in the past, and it seems that their reaction to him was a bit defensive. Paul did respond with more instruction, but also with more sensitivity and vulnerability:

> We put no stumbling block in anyone's path, so that our ministry will not be discredited. Rather, as servants of God we commend ourselves in every way: in great endurance; in troubles, hardships and distresses; in beatings, imprisonments and riots; in hard work, sleepless nights and hunger; in purity, understanding, patience and kindness; in the Holy Spirit and in sincere love; in truthful speech and in the power of God; with weapons of righteousness in the right hand and in the left; through glory and dishonor, bad report and good report; genuine, yet regarded as impostors; known, yet regarded as unknown; dying, and yet we live on; beaten, and yet not killed; sorrowful, yet always rejoicing; poor, yet making many rich; having nothing, and yet possessing everything.
>
> We have spoken freely to you, Corinthians, and opened wide our hearts to you. We are not withholding our affection from you, but you are withholding yours from us. As a fair exchange—I speak as to my children—open wide your hearts also (2 Cor. 6:3-13).

Why did Paul reveal his pain? What was his purpose? I am sure he had several things in mind, but one major lesson we can learn from this letter is that Christians go through difficult times.

Throughout the writings of Paul, it is obvious that the teacher and evangelist was, himself, acquainted with pain of all shapes and sizes. Yet he didn't try to pretend that the suffering didn't matter. He didn't try to go it alone. Instead, he reached out and asked for the support of the ones he loved and needed most.

Paul gave us the legacy of a church involved with one another. He modeled a father-son relationship with Timothy (Phil. 2:19-24; 1, 2 Tim.); brotherhood relationships with Epaphroditus (Phil. 2:25-30), Onesimus (Phile.), Barnabas (Acts 9:26-27), Priscilla and Aquila (Acts 18), Crispus (Acts 18), and many others. He modeled open relationships with people in all of the churches united in the name of Jesus Christ.

When one church had a financial need, Paul encouraged others to take part (2 Cor. 9). He urged the members of the church to love one another, to discipline and correct one another toward godliness, to comfort one another in need and in pain, to take care of the widows and the orphans in their midst, to share with those in need, and to worship the living God side by side.

Paul lived with his heart opened wide, and he longed for the members of the church to do the same.

### Comfort in the Church
The remainder of this book will outline a philosophy, a program, and a plan for caregiving in the church. There is certainly a need, and we have the resources and the bodies to effectively meet that need.

While it is true that there are already a number of social organizations that are more than willing to shoulder the load, there is simply no substitution for Christ's love in the church. We may have to learn a few new skills and open our minds to some new ideas, but the essence of the program lies in the love that characterizes the church throughout the world.

We have much to offer those who love God, and much more, in turn, to offer a hurting world.

# SECTION TWO:
# Exploring the Ministry
# of Comfort

Praise be to the God and Father of our Lord Jesus Christ, the Father of compassion and the God of all comfort, who comforts us in all our troubles, so that we can comfort those in any trouble with the comfort we ourselves have received from God. For just as the sufferings of Christ flow over into our lives, so also through Christ our comfort overflows. If we are distressed, it is for your comfort and salvation; if we are comforted, it is for your comfort, which produces in you patient endurance of the same sufferings we suffer. And our hope for you is firm, because we know that just as you share in our sufferings, so also you share in our comfort.

2 Corinthians 1:3-7

# FOUR

## The Comfort We
## Have Received

Have you ever wanted God to tell you what He's going to do? Have you ever just wanted five minutes with Him to receive an answer or two to those pressing questions? Perhaps you've longed just to be with Him for a moment to enjoy His comfort.

I remember my early years of faith. I attended a school where being a Christian wasn't very popular, so I was always a bit lonely. People didn't seem to understand the most important part of my life, and I hungered for some way to express my commitment and feelings.

The end of the day was always my most creative time. As I sat and played the guitar well into the new morning, my thoughts would turn to this great and glorious God I longed to know.

It was at those moments that I would pray for just one visit from my Savior. I recall promising never to ask again, if He would just come and sit by my bed for one brief moment.

I don't know if you've allowed yourself the same musings, but I do know that most of us would cherish the chance to spend some time alone with God—whether it be for conversation or just for a good cry. We long for His comfort in a world that is so very uncomfortable at times.

### From Out of the Storm
In the early days of my bout with cancer, I felt very alone. I spoke with God again and again, but I didn't hear a response. I wanted to know why He had allowed the illness and what He

was going to do about my pain. I wanted some answers to some very difficult questions.

Job too demanded answers. In fact, he spoke so loudly that everyone could hear him. Where once he had been a well-respected man about town, he found himself in the company of ashes and painful boils. Where once others had sought his counsel, suffering left him friendless and hounded by those with "sound" advice.

I believe Job began his transformation somewhere around chapter 10. Up to that point, he had been doing a lot of talking about God and the possible reasons for his loss. He, as I, had tried to speculate and reason, but to no avail.

In chapter 10, however, we see a subtle change take place. Instead of talking about God and the situation, Job began talking to God. Granted, his words were full of despair, but at least they were personally addressed! He opened up a channel that would prove to be full of life.

Many of us wouldn't dare to say the things Job said. We probably wouldn't even admit to thinking them. But Job had little to lose. And so he spoke . . . and spoke . . . and questioned . . . and pitied himself. He felt useless and used; directionless and lost.

Time passed, and after much growth we see a ray of light spring from Job's eyes as he gave witness to the fact that his Redeemer lives (Job 19:23-27). From the bottom of the pit Job had at least climbed to ground level. And then came the interaction he had been praying for. Out of a brewing storm came a sonorous voice, putting an end to Job's seclusion.

What do you suppose Job wanted to hear from God? What do you want to hear in those dark moments? I have often read the story and supplied my own version of God's response to His suffering servant. The conversation I imagine goes something like this: "Job, My dear servant. I know how much you've been suffering and how difficult life has been for you all these months. I don't know how you were able to make it this far. Why, I can't imagine anyone going through what you've faced with any more courage."

Does this sound familiar? Be honest for a moment. Haven't you ever wanted to hear those words directed your way (with a personal touch, of course)? Haven't you dreamed of God holding you up as an example of fortitude and righteousness in the midst of battle? I have. God did speak to Job. He just used different words.

Since the fall of 1982, I have read Job 38–42 daily. In fact, I guess I have memorized the soliloquy by now. God didn't use the language I invented, but a perspective of His own. Let me summarize the monologue: "Job, My servant, you've been doing a great deal of talking in recent months. And if you don't mind My saying so, you've been speaking much about that which you know very little. Didn't I create the world? Haven't I given you breath? Have I ever lost control? Am I not faithful to Myself? Have I not been faithful to you? Do you have any reason to believe that I've changed? Job, My servant, remember . . . I AM."

## The Comfort We Have Received

You'll forgive me if this sounds too simplistic, but we don't have to look very far to discover the comfort we've received. God revealed Himself to Job. His creative genius, His faithful love, His commitment to humanity, His sovereignty are so evident all around us and in us. He comforts us all the time. We just have to learn to see through His eyes.

How has God comforted you recently? How has He soothed your pain? How has He responded to your heart calls? How has He revealed His unfailing love?

Let me offer some ideas:

A *Friendly Voice*. One way God comforts us is through the love of our friends. Few things can cheer us more than a visit from someone we hold dear.

I'll never forget waking up from my first surgery. I was in greater pain than I had ever known or could have imagined. I knew something was wrong, but it hurt so much to breathe that I didn't have the energy to ask.

I remember shivering and shaking and not being able to feel warm. And I remember unfamiliar faces calling, "Mary, are you awake? Mary?" They didn't seem to know that I've gone by the name of "Shelley" since a little girl. They didn't know me. Their job was to care for my body.

Then came the sea of loving faces. They were faces in pain, as they had just been told of my cancer. But they were faces of

37

love—faces I had known and felt comfortable with for years.

The comfort of my friends didn't stop there. Day after day they came to the hospital. And after I was ushered home, they stopped by and cried with me, or helped me do some menial task.

One way God comforts us is through those who love us "as they love themselves."

*Creation.* I don't know about you, but I can be feeling terrible and then see a sunset, different in its splendor from ever before. In that moment of beauty I can find my bearings and realize that God is still in control.

One way that God comforts us is through the world that He has made for our enjoyment. When we see it "in the raw," His creation is spectacular.

How does the sun rise and set each day, bringing us such stability and warmth? How does that moon take on so many lovely shapes and sizes? And what can be more breathtaking than brilliant stars on a dark night?

Do you sense an overwhelming peace when the waves wash up on the shore? Do the birds flying overhead offer a reminder of freedom? Does the intricate delicacy of a rose bring memories of your own beauty in God's eyes?

Sometimes, when all else seems blurred, our vision is restored through a view of God's creation.

*God's Word.* I don't think I have ever opened the Word of God and been disappointed in my findings. In fact, I can read a passage over and over and still find new life and new meaning.

God's Word is filled with wisdom, with instruction, with comfort, with poetry, with steadfast love and purpose. And if we are simply in need of "connecting" with someone who has felt the pains we are feeling, there are vignettes of suffering and hearts poured out to God.

His Word is not empty or flat. Instead, there is layer after layer of meaning and guidance. It is as if God has written a personal message of comfort and strength for each of us. He comforts us through His truth.

*Forgiveness.* I became a Christian at an early age, so I was not too aware of my own sinfulness. In the general sense I knew I fell short of God's glory, but I wasn't too sure how such a condition worked itself out in my daily life.

Then came the day when I knew so well that I needed His forgiveness. There is nothing I wanted more than to please Him, yet I couldn't seem to find the right ingredients for my longing. I discovered my sin and the painful expression that it wears. And then I understood.

When Jesus introduced Simon to the prostitute in Luke 7, He introduced her as a woman who knew how to love. What did He mean?

She had been forgiven much, Jesus said; therefore she knew a great deal about love. As she washed His feet with her hair, love poured into that room.

When we've been believers for a while, we grow accustomed to our own sins. In fact, they become so much like "old shoes" that we barely notice them anymore. Other people's sins, however, are a different matter. We see the splinters in other people's eyes quite clearly.

Sometimes God humbles and comforts us by washing us with His sweet aroma of forgiveness. He reminds us of our battle with sin, but even more He reminds us of the One who is ultimately victorious in that battle.

In recent years, I have prayed to see my sins more and more clearly. It has been a difficult prayer to pray, yet an interesting one to have answered.

God has been gently showing me the struggles of my heart, and just as gently offering His forgiveness and love. What a comforting agent His forgiveness can be, if we'll put aside the pride and open our eyes to such healing.

*Groanings Too Deep for Words.* I attended a large Episcopal church as a child. The sanctuary was beautifully adorned with stained glass windows and a large stone altar. Cherubim and archangels were carved into a large marble face on the front wall. When you entered the sanctuary, an immediate sense of awe filled your being.

I was alone most Sundays. Feeling a bit small and unsure of myself, I immediately latched onto a man who sat one pew in front of me. When he sang, I sang. When he stood, I stood. When he knelt, I knelt. And most of the time, things went well.

What I recall most, however, was a frustrated effort to pay attention during prayer. The Episcopal service had many places where prayer was central to the worship, but I was young, and my attention span was not very long.

I remember apologizing to God for losing my train of thought. And I remember trying time and again to make it through the prayer with careful concentration. I don't think I succeeded at my goal very often.

When I came to know the Lord, several years later, one of the first joys was the discovery of prayer. It seemed that suddenly my prayers had meaning, and I wasn't struggling to stay on the subject. I had much to learn about prayer, but immediately it seemed so personal.

As the years passed, I began to experience the joy of just conversing with God. In the shower, in my bed, in class, through tears, on a walk outside, or listening to music, I could pray. And the prayer didn't have to end with an "Amen."

I could even pray when words didn't come or when I felt unsure of how to talk with God. Whether lonely or frightened, grateful or loved, I could tell that the Spirit was praying for me with yearnings too deep for words (Rom. 8:26-27). My heartfelt expressions were reaching my Father, and His love was reaching me.

One of the most beautiful gifts God has given us lies in the privilege of talking with Him whenever we want as long as we want about anything that's on our minds. What comfort!

He comforts us through our ability to communicate with Him and through His reciprocal longing to communicate with us.

### "Let Me Count the Ways"
I have explored only a few of the ways God comforts me—ways that we'll examine more closely in the chapters that follow. I pray that the glimpses into my life will challenge you to discover the many ways He has reached out to you in your pain.

The kind of comfort we share is directly related to our awareness of God's comfort in our lives. Explore the ways He ministers to you so that you can share His comforts with others in need.

# FIVE

## Jesus' Ministry of Comfort

Jesus walked this earth spreading love and sharing comfort. Just like today, the world in which Jesus lived was a world filled with suffering and loss, confusion and violence, selfishness and prejudice. The people needed comfort then just as we do now, and He had much to give away to those who sought His relief. Remember the words we so often hear in times of need:

> Come to Me, all you who are weary and burdened, and I will give you rest. Take My yoke upon you and learn from Me, for I am gentle and humble in heart, and you will find rest for your souls. For My yoke is easy and My burden is light (Matt. 11:28-30).

Do His words comfort you? Do you sense that Jesus' burden is light? Are there times when His comfort seems to elude you? Does rest ever seem an illusion?

We make a mistake to assume that those words were spoken in some quiet moment of kindness when there was no conflict brewing. Instead, Jesus spoke those words right after pronouncing "woe" on the cities in which most of His miracles had already been performed (vv. 20-24).

> Woe to you, Korazin! Woe to you, Bethsaida! If the miracles that were performed in you had been performed in Tyre and Sidon, they would have repented

> long ago in sackcloth and ashes. But I tell you, it will
> be more bearable for Tyre and Sidon on the day of
> judgment than for you (vv. 21-22).

Since many people were rejecting our Lord, He had to speak the truth to them about their rejection. It was in the wake of such difficult times that Jesus spoke first with His Father (vv. 25-26) and then to all who would hear, "Come to Me."

It is difficult for us to understand how Jesus could speak words of comfort right after pronouncements that were anything but comfortable. We are a people who do not value conflict and pain. In fact, we go to great lengths to avoid suffering or to lessen and shorten its blows.

Jesus seemed to be "at peace" with the fact that suffering does and will exist and that it actually has a purpose. Such a concept isn't easy for us to grasp.

We are a "doing" society, not a "being" society. When someone offers comfort for our pain, we immediately look for relief from that pain. We might think, for example, that for Jesus to offer comfort in Matthew 11, He would have to undo or resolve the woes against the cities. Having both woe and comfort at the same time just doesn't seem to mix.

Think, for a moment, about our advertisements. Picture the man with heartburn. How does he spell relief? R-O-L-A-I-D-S. What about the woman with a terrible headache? How does she spell relief? A-S-P-I-R-I-N. And how is relief spelled when last season's automobile is giving us trouble? N-E-W-C-A-R. Do you see what I mean?

We are a society that expects a comforting agent to remove the problem, preferably without our having to change any habits or alter our lifestyles. Is it any wonder, then, that when we look to God for comfort—when we *pray* to God for comfort—we anticipate the removal of the suffering? Perhaps this is one reason we are confused when the pain continues.

Jesus offered comfort to the hurting people of this world. Sometimes His comfort was the removal of one aspect of pain, but that was neither His purpose nor His promise. Rather than committing Himself to placing us under constant protection from all pain, He promised comfort, purpose, and strength in the midst of that pain.

42

The removal of suffering, frequent as it was in Jesus' ministry, was a point-in-time event. People heard about this great Man, and they desired His miracles because He saw their suffering and had compassion on them.

Yet even Jesus made it clear that the real "bread and water" He had to offer were not the ones made from flour or drawn from a well (John 6). The real miracles He had to offer, and still offers, come from the inside out.

Jesus' comfort includes pain, it does not demand or command the removal of all suffering. Perhaps a closer look at Jesus' ministry will further reveal His methods of offering comfort to a hurting world.

### Upside Down—Right Side Up

When Jesus took the disciples across the lake into the region of the Decapolis (Mark 5:1-20), His public ministry had already begun. It was now time to spread the Word to another group of people who needed to hear. Though the boat ride was uneventful, the arrival was anything but.

After our Lord reached the shore and got out of the boat, a man with an evil spirit came up to Him. The man had been living in the tombs for years, unsuccessfully chained and amply feared by all. His life was upside down, and no one seemed to care.

So often in this world, the ones who need our help the most are the very ones we find distasteful. We want people to find some kind of support, but most of us don't want to be the person who delivers that support. Working with "upside down" people isn't very comfortable—even if we've faced the identical struggle at some point in our own lives.

The man with an evil spirit had an obvious need. He needed freedom from the intruder who had taken up residence in his heart. Jesus readily answered that need, driving the demons into a herd of pigs and over a cliff. For the first time in a long time, the man was whole—right side up. But that wasn't the end of his treatment.

People in the neighborhood weren't thrilled with Jesus' concern. After all, to save one man no one cared about, Jesus sacrificed the livelihood of the local herdsmen. They wanted Jesus gone, and our Lord adhered to that request.

43

"Let me go with You," begged the newly delivered man. "Let me go and serve You along with the others."

"No, go home to your family," was Jesus' reply. "Go home to your family and tell them all that the Lord has done for you." And with that Jesus crossed to the other side of the lake.

I can picture the scene. Can you? Jesus pulling away from the shore, the man waving a fond good-bye to the One who had made his life livable again.

Jesus comforted the man on one level by casting out the demon and turning his world right side up, but that wasn't the extent of the comfort. Without giving the man a new way to live, the first gift would have made little difference.

When Jesus sent the man back home, He comforted him by giving him responsibility. Think about his trip home for a moment. For the first time in a long time, the man walked down the street with dignity. He had a story to tell that could transform lives. He had friends to make and love, advice to give, a memorable moment to keep alive, a Savior to glorify.

Jesus comforted the man in a way that outlasted the excitement of a miraculous moment. He comforted the man with the gift of responsibility and the respect that such a gift brings.

Sometimes comforting someone means giving them responsibility for and with their lives. Jesus knew the importance of such comfort.

### The Healing Power of Touch

Mark 5 also tells the story of a woman who had suffered for twelve long years. She had a physical condition that subjected her to bleeding; and as if that weren't enough, the fact that she was bleeding and a woman made her untouchable by the world in which she lived (Lev. 15:19-30).

Most of us, when we are ill, relish the attention of family members and friends. We want our loved ones close, and a simple touch, hug, or kiss can make such a difference. Since suffering often makes us feel untouchable, we need the concern of others to remind us of our worth.

The woman knew no such concern. We are told that she spent all of her money searching for a medical cure, and I imagine that people avoided her almost everywhere she went. She had little left to hope for—until she learned that Jesus was in her town, near her home, sharing with people she knew.

We are given enough clues from the passage to piece together a scant picture of the events of this miraculous meeting. The woman had a game plan for carrying out the fulfillment of her hope. If she could just touch Jesus' robes from behind, all would be well. He wouldn't even have to know!

In a carefully chosen moment, while Jesus was being ushered off to heal the daughter of a religious man, the woman crept into the picture and reached out to touch the edge of His garments. At once, she was healed of her physical disease.

"Who touched Me?" Jesus asked as He turned to those crowded around Him.

"We're all touching You," replied the disciples, anxious for Jesus to hurry up and help the "important" religious leader.

"No, this touch was different," Jesus said, and His eyes focused on the woman's fear and shame.

Again, at first glance we see the physical healing as comfort. And it was a tremendous gift. The healing brought her freedom from twelve long years of pain. But something else happened in that vulnerable moment. Jesus comforted her by accepting her as she was—"untouchable" in the eyes of the world, yet worthy of touch by Him.

Had the woman come in contact with any other religious leaders, she would have been shamed and scolded. To touch a bleeding woman was to be rendered "unclean." Any leader coming in contact with her would have to go through the purification rituals before becoming acceptable once again. As we might imagine, the woman was shunned for her unclean ways.

Yet Jesus didn't scold her for touching His garments. He didn't become "unclean" because of her need. Instead of chastising the woman, our Lord listened to her story, called her "daughter," welcomed her touch, and accepted her just as she was.

"Just as I am, without one plea, but that Thy blood was shed for Me. And that Thou bidst me come to Thee, O Lamb of God, I come—I come" ("Just As I Am," Charlotte Elliott, 1834).

Sometimes the comfort someone needs is found in that great combination gift of touch and acceptance. When we reach out to someone and love the person exactly where he or she is, we offer a comfort that transforms.

This woman had a new reason to live. She was no longer the "untouchable" one; she belonged. She had been heard and welcomed in the midst of her pain.

### "Just Believe"

There are few words more difficult to hear than: "Just believe." Most of us want to believe when times are hard, but it's just not that simple. When we are hurt or afraid, believing takes all of the courage we can muster.

Jairus was a leader among the Jewish ruling class. He was a synagogue ruler; a job that required much responsibility.

Jairus' duties included organizing the worship service at the synagogue, selecting the men who would read God's Word or speak the prayers, and generally overseeing the duties and programs at the house of worship (*New Bible Dictionary*, 2nd edition [Wheaton, Ill.: Tyndale House Publishers, 1982], p. 549). He had, no doubt, heard of Jesus; and I'm certain he knew that Jesus was not a popular man among the Jewish leaders.

We are introduced to Jairus in the Gospel of Mark when he approached Jesus, pleading with our Lord for help.

"My little daughter is dying," Jairus explained. "Please come and put Your hand on her so that she will be healed and live" (Mark 5:21-24, 35-43).

Isn't it amazing how easy it is to scoff at someone until we need that person's help? Before his little daughter became ill, Jairus was probably suspicious of the activities of this new Prophet and Teacher. When someone he dearly loved was dying, however, Jairus not only asked for Jesus' help, he knelt at Jesus' feet. Jesus, of course, agreed to go with him to the side of his little daughter.

It was at this time that the woman, bleeding for twelve years, approached our Lord and touched Him. Imagine yourself as Jairus for a moment—a father whose little daughter was at the point of death. In Jairus' world, a bleeding woman was unworthy of Jesus' time. Jairus as a Jewish leader deserved the attention, didn't he?

Just as Jesus finished working with the woman, messengers arrived to tell Jairus not to bother the Teacher anymore. His daughter had died; there was nothing left to do. And Jairus' heart fell hard.

"Don't be afraid." Jesus' words pierced through the grief. "Don't be afraid, just believe."

I can almost see Jairus looking at Jesus with anything but belief. What did He mean, just believe? Believe in what?

We know that Jesus could have spoken the word and sent Jairus home to a healthy daughter. We know too that Jesus allowed Jairus to struggle with faith during the long walk home.

Only Jairus, Peter, James, and John were allowed to accompany Jesus to the house of the synagogue ruler. I imagine Jairus was in shock, hungering not for a miracle but for some comfort from the pain.

How do you accept the death of a child? Would she have been spared had the woman not interrupted them? What would he say to his wife? The language of grief is universal.

When they reached the house, everyone was crying until Jesus "shook things up" with a simple statement: "Why all this commotion and wailing? The child is not dead but asleep" (Mark 5:39). No one knew what to say.

And then the Comforter walked in. Jesus spoke healing words and helped the young girl stand. Without even a difficult recovery, she was up and walking around the room. To everyone's surprise, life had begun again.

We would label raising the girl from the dead as the comfort of Jesus. And, surely, comfort was found in that generous act of compassion. But the comfort started earlier and lasted much, much longer. Remember the words, "Don't be afraid, just believe"? Sometimes comfort is found in giving someone the chance to grow in faith. Jesus gave Jairus that chance.

Why did Jesus make Jairus wait? Why did He require Jairus to go through the motions? Why did Jairus have to watch as the woman received her touch? Why, indeed?

Faith is all about waiting, about believing, about accompanying Jesus, about selflessness and trust. Faith is all about "just believing." Jesus comforted Jairus in one great way by healing his daughter. But Jesus comforted Jairus eternally by granting him the privilege to learn about faith.

### The Perspective of Jesus
While we seek comfort so often in the removal of the outside pain, Jesus sees comfort as the maturing of the inside man or

woman. While we seek comfort in temporal and physical terms, Jesus sees comfort in internal and eternal terms.

The beginning of coming to grips with the many faces of comfort lies in our attitude. If we seek comfort as the removal of pain, our lives will be predictable and, eventually, disappointing. If we seek comfort in its many layers, our lives will be full and satisfying.

Jesus exhibited so many aspects of comfort. He knew His people well, and He knew their fears and their wants. Yet He also knew exactly what they needed to grow in all aspects into Him. He still knows exactly what we need.

Thank God that He cares so very much about who we are becoming. The many faces of comfort reflect the many faces of our Savior's love.

# SIX

## The Many Faces
## of Comfort

When Paul spoke of comfort to the Corinthians, he spoke from years of experience and deep awareness of God's comfort in his own life.

How does God comfort you? Think about it. Make the list. Be aware of the methods God has used through the years to bring comfort in your sorrow. Look past the removal of difficulty to the strength that He offers to bear the difficulty and grow from its lessons.

The Gospels are full of examples of Jesus extending comfort to people in need. In fact, God's Word includes enumerable stories of comfort being given and received. We've already looked at some of God's offerings, but there are many more to explore.

If we see the stories merely on their surface, then we learn to define comfort as the absence of pain. If we see lives in their richness, then we learn to see comfort with its many faces.

### Touch

As we saw with the woman in Mark 5, touch can play such an important role in a hurting person's life. We feel unlovable when we are hurting—a crumb cast out of the society in which we live.

When a loved one dies, when we hear the diagnosis of cancer, when a child leaves home angry and undirected, when divorce ends a marriage once planned for life, when aging sets in, when physical pain becomes a daily reality, when we feel disappointed with God—when these things happen, we need the touch of someone who cares. We need to feel accepted and understood, just as we are.

One face of comfort is the face of touch. Few simple gestures can provide more strength and love than touch.

While in Belize, Central America, one Thanksgiving, I was asked to visit a young girl who was dying from cancer of the lung. I knew very little about her before reaching the hospital, so when I saw her I was immediately taken back. She wasn't just dying, she was hanging on by merely a thread.

Carly had been in the hospital ward for over six weeks. Only two weeks after her admission, Carly's parents had walked out, saying they were unable to watch her die in this way. Until I walked in, Carly had seen few visitors and known no comforts of touch.

Normally, I would have rushed to the side of this sixteen-year-old and taken her into my arms, but fear complicated the situation. Carly's arms and face were blotched with bleeding sores, and her diseased skin lay beside her on the bed. I knew she needed touch, but I was afraid to reach out.

I drew as close to the young girl as I could without coming in actual contact with her. Carly's breathing was labored; her lips cracked.

I talked to her about my own experiences with cancer, about the normal feelings of fear and loneliness, about Jesus and His death and life, about heaven. But no matter how warmly I spoke, she avoided my eyes. The battle within me began.

One voice inside said, "Touch her." The other, more cautious, said, "You'd better be careful!" By God's grace, my heart won the debate, and I carefully picked Carly up and held her close.

For the first time since our meeting began, Carly looked right into my eyes and we both began to cry. Can you imagine how unlovable that young girl felt, slowly facing death without the support of a family.

I don't know how long she remained in my arms, but I know that touch bridged a gap where words had failed. We met in the world of the heart the day before she died.

Carly accepted Christ into her heart that day, and now she lives with Jesus, whole and very touchable. She's been welcomed into the presence of the King, and she stands beautiful and strong for eternity.

Whether it's stroking someone's hair, holding a person who's crying, or giving a much-needed hug, touch speaks one thousand words of acceptance and understanding.

### Forgiveness

Sometimes comfort's face is one of forgiveness. Hurting someone else or being hurt can be such a devastating experience. Such pain is hard to forgive, much less to forget.

One of the most painful times in Peter's life occurred in the final hours of our Lord's time on earth. Peter had vowed to protect Jesus — to keep Him from harm (Matt. 16:22); yet in our Lord's time of need, Peter let Him down (26:69-75). Broken and unable to do anything about the guilt, Peter joined the others in the Upper Room and waited — for what, they weren't sure.

Can you imagine Peter's feelings during the three days our Lord rested in the tomb? How could he make peace with Jesus? If only he could have said, "I'm sorry." Instead, life was more frightening than ever before, and Jesus wasn't there to tell them what to do.

Enter the risen Lord, ready, once again, to walk with His disciples and prepare them for the task ahead. While Peter was thrilled with the reunion, he didn't know what to say. This was all too wonderful . . . and humbling!

The end of the Gospel of John records a sensitive scene of forgiveness and restoration. Jesus had taught the disciples, prepared them for their futures, and opened the Scriptures for their understanding. Still, a sort of pain existed between Himself and Peter.

> When they had finished eating, Jesus said to Simon Peter, "Simon son of John, do you truly love Me more than these?"
>
> "Yes, Lord," he said, "You know that I love You."
>
> Jesus said, "Feed My lambs."
>
> Again Jesus said, "Simon son of John, do you truly love Me?"
>
> He answered, "Yes, Lord, You know that I love You."

Jesus said, "Take care of My sheep."
The third time He said to him, "Simon son of John, do you love Me?"
Peter was hurt because Jesus asked him the third time, "Do you love Me?" He said, "Lord, You know all things; You know that I love You."
Jesus said, "Feed My sheep" (John 20:15-17).

Jesus had suffered greatly because of Peter's betrayal. We all hurt the people we love at times, and we can all feel Peter's guilt.

Peter was hurt too. He longed for the past to be behind him. He wanted to get on with the business of serving Christ. He did not want to face his denial once again.

Jesus could have avoided the previous painful incident, but that is not how our Lord works. His comfort doesn't pass over the problem, it passes through.

Though rehashing the incident was painful to Peter, the issue was out in the open and finished, though not forgotten. It would become a teaching point for Peter from that day on, as he shared the comfort of forgiveness with people in Jerusalem, in Judea, and even to the ends of the earth.

Whether we're directly involved with someone's pain or not, we can offer the forgiveness that comes through Jesus Christ and through love for one another. Sometimes what people need the most is the comfort of knowing they're forgiven.

### Responsibility

One face of comfort lies in helping people take responsibility for their lives. Jesus gave this gift to the man in Mark 5, and it was a very strategic one.

When we are hurting, we tend to want to "give up." We prefer for people and life to pass us by and leave us in our pain. Instead, it is best to hold on to life and to the responsibilities God has given.

Two of my favorite stories contrast the lame man in John 5 with the blind man in John 9. Both were sufferers, both were outcasts, both were healed by Jesus on the Sabbath Day, and both were given opportunity to make something of their lives.

The man in John 5 had suffered for thirty-eight years. We

know that he was partially paralyzed, and we know that he had few friends who were there to lower him into the pool when the water was stirred.

When Jesus encountered the man, He asked an interesting question. Seeing the man by the pool at Bethsaida, He asked, "Do you want to get well?" What a strange question to ask a person who is lame! Why wouldn't he want to get well? Especially after thirty-eight long years?

"No one is here to help me," was the man's reply. Do you see? He did not say, "Yes"; he said, in effect, "There's nothing I can do about my own situation." Apparently Jesus didn't agree. He healed the man and sent him away to live his new life.

The story is a tragic one, but eerily familiar. The man picked up his bed and left the pool, but not with joy. He didn't thank Jesus for His help. He wasn't curious to find out who Jesus was or why He had chosen to offer healing. The man simply left and remained discontent.

When the Pharisees inquired as to why he was carrying his bed on the Sabbath, the man did not say, "Isn't this great? I'm whole! Let me introduce you to the wonderful Man who helped me." Sadly, he simply said, "The Man who healed me told me to pick up my bed." Nothing more—no joy, no purpose. It is little wonder that Jesus sought him out once more to say, "Stop sinning, or something worse may happen to you."

Jesus removed the initial reason for the man's complaint, but in so doing revealed the heart of the man himself. He didn't want to be better. He wanted an excuse to be miserable and helpless. The comfort Jesus had given him was responsibility— and he didn't like it one bit.

The blind man in John 9 is a totally different story. He too was a beggar with a reason to complain, until Jesus put saliva in his eyes and told him to go and wash. Coming out of the water, the man could see! For the first time, he had vision.

He too was persecuted unduly by the Pharisees. He too was questioned about Jesus' unlawful activities on the Sabbath. But there was a great difference in the blind man's reply.

As the Pharisees questioned, the man born blind became stronger and more courageous and much more responsible. He didn't know who or where Jesus was, but he stood up for the Lord and honored Him before men.

The story is a fascinating one. We might think the man a theologian by his replies! He put the Pharisees in their places and seemed not to care that his newfound responsibility was making enemies right and left. Not even his parents had the courage to stand up to the religious leaders.

When Jesus found this man again, He didn't find a blind beggar with no purpose in life other than waiting by the road for coins. He found, instead, a man with a longing to know God.

Jesus offered the comfort of physical healing to both men, but both did not welcome the comfort of responsibility. One was content to remain ill with an excuse. Only one was willing to grow and accept a new reason for living.

Our most natural response to someone in pain is to remove that person's responsibility. For a brief time, such is often a much appreciated gesture. But even the dying person does best when allowed to remain responsible for portions of his or her life.

Be creative in your comfort. Help people learn to take responsibility for and with the life that is theirs. Though it is tempting to take over and protect, responsibility is an important component to any person's well-being.

**Prayer**

I chose this aspect of comfort because it is often put off until all of our own efforts appear fruitless. Prayer is a function of "being" rather than "doing," and it is very difficult for you and me to stop the "doing" in times of need.

So often, when we pray for someone else, we pray for the removal of suffering, not for insight in its midst. Think back to a recent prayer meeting you've attended or a recent time of intercession in your own closet. How have the prayer requests been handled? What have you petitioned from God? What is your working definition of "answered prayer"?

A beautiful passage of Scripture begins in John 14 and concludes with a time of prayer in John 17. Jesus was preparing His disciples for His own death, and, in so doing, prayed for their courage, strength, and direction in days to come.

I think it is important to note that Jesus didn't remove His disciples from temptations, pains, struggles, or the hate of this world. In fact, in His prayer He fully acknowledged the above.

What He prayed for was their unity, their protection from Satan by the power of God's name, their sanctification by the Word, and their continued growing knowledge of God and God's love. What better to gird them with than eternal comforts?

People who are hurting need to be prayed for *and* prayed with. We lose sight of how to pray at times. We lose sight of what to pray for at times. We need to search for the essence of God's perspective rather than simply offering a prayer for the removal of pain. It is difficult to pray with such faith, but the strength that accompanies that prayer is greater than the weakness dealt by any form of pain.

Sometimes God will elect to remove physically the suffering. Sometimes He will grant immediate relief from the emotional strain of depression or grief. But that is not the way He always works, nor is such relief *better* than His provision of strength, love, and perspective in the midst of the storm.

Use the Psalms, Lamentations, passages of honesty here and there, and help people pour out their hearts before God. The result of such outpouring is the comfort that only prayer can bring.

## The God of All Comfort

"Praise be to the God and Father of our Lord Jesus Christ, the Father of compassion and the God of all comfort" (2 Cor. 1:3).

We have seen a few faces of comfort in depth: faces of touch, of forgiveness, of responsibility, of prayer; but those aren't the only methods God uses to comfort you and me in our need.

It is so difficult for us to look past the "doing" activities that characterize our relationships. If someone is ill, we think about what we can "do" to help. We might visit at the hospital or take meals; we might offer to keep the children or run errands. But whatever we do, we generally feel that we're helping only if we're "doing." What Scripture tries to teach us about God's comfort is that it far surpasses activity—it is a function of God's "being."

Sometimes, comfort is just "being with." Remember when Jesus asked the disciples to accompany Him in His last moments of prayer in the Garden? (Matt. 26:36-46; Luke 22:39-46) He didn't want anything from them, so to speak—merely their pres-

55

ence. Struggling people long for our presence—for us just to "be with" them.

Sometimes, comfort is crying with the person in pain. Jesus demonstrated such sensitivity with Mary at the loss of her brother and His close friend. Even though He knew that He would soon raise Lazarus from the dead, He took the time to cry with Mary (John 11:29-35).

Sometimes, people long for us to know them and accept them as they are. This face of comfort is difficult, yet often so important. Our sins separate us, and it takes sensitivity to bring those who are sinning into fellowship and renewal.

Think, for a moment, of the woman at the well (4:4-26) and the adulteress who narrowly escaped stoning (8:1-11). Jesus didn't condemn their sin, though He made it clear that they needed a change in their lives. He accepted them as they were and counted them worthy of love.

Sometimes, comfort comes in the sharing of truth itself—the great eternal gift of God. Truth is the gift Jesus shared with His disciples as He prepared them for His death (John 14–16).

He did not promise to remove all obstacles or to relieve all suffering, but He did give them truth about what they could expect from this world and from Him. He promised that they would grieve His absence and be hated by the world. He promised the Spirit. He promised strength. He promised to return. Jesus comforted those He loved with His truth.

How has God comforted you? Through your friends? Through a timely lesson or sermon? Through a welcomed letter, card, or phone call? Through a song? Through a sunset? Through His Word? Through a glimpse at the purpose of our suffering? Through responsibility? Through forgiveness? Through patience?

There are so many faces of comfort, and they run deep. Believers have lived by God's comfort for years, and it is that same comfort that people need from the church—within her walls. We need to comfort one another with the same comfort we ourselves have received. There is no greater gift.

# SECTION THREE:
## Dealing with Grief and Depression

I am the man who has seen affliction by the rod of His wrath. He has driven me away and made we walk in darkness rather than light;
Indeed, He has turned His hand against me again and again, all day long.
He has made my skin and my flesh grow old and has broken my bones.
He has besieged and surrounded me with bitterness and hardship.
He has made me dwell in darkness like those long dead.
He has walled me in so I cannot escape; He has weighed me down with chains.
Even when I call out or cry for help, He shuts out my prayer.
He has barred my way with blocks of stone; He has made my paths crooked.
Like a bear lying in wait, like a lion in hiding, He dragged me from the path and mangled me and left me without help.
He drew His bow and made me the target for His arrows.
He pierced my heart with arrows from His quiver.
I became the laughingstock of all my people; they mock me in song all day long.
He has filled me with bitter herbs and sated me with gall.
He has broken my teeth with gravel; He has trampled me in the dust.

I have been deprived of peace; I have forgotten what prosperity is.
So I say, "My splendor is gone and all that I had hoped from the Lord."
I remember my affliction and my wandering, the bitterness and the gall.
I well remember them, and my soul is downcast within me.
Yet this I call to mind and therefore I have hope:
Because of the Lord's great love we are not consumed, for His compassions never fail.
They are new every morning; great is Your faithfulness.

Lamentations 3:1-23

# SEVEN

## The Colorful World
## of Emotions

What a great gift God has given us through our emotions. They are like a well deep within us from which we draw expressions of response, need, change, and expectation. Emotions are part of being created in the image of God.

It is often said and taught that certain emotions are "negative" and, thus, unhealthy and suspect. For a moment, make a list of all those emotions that might go on your "negative" list: emotions such as anger, depression, jealousy, guilt, hatred. Does this sound familiar?

I readily agree that living with unresolved emotions can have a negative effect on our lives. I also agree that what we do with certain emotions can reap a negative harvest. But emotions, in and of themselves, are not the culprits and need not be suspected of wrongdoing. Emotions aren't "positive" or "negative," they simply "are." They are our heart's response to the various aspects of living in this world.

### The Way We Feel
The most natural response to circumstances lies in the seat of our emotions. When we watch a movie with a sad ending, we cry. When we see a story on the news about rape or murder, we become angry or afraid.

When someone we love is cruel or insensitive, we become hurt. When our husband, wife, mother, or father turn their affections on someone else, we feel jealous and left out.

When someone tells untruths about us or misrepresents what we've said, we feel frustrated and betrayed. The list can go on and on and on.

Is it wrong or negative to be angry when someone is raped? Is it wrong or negative to be angry when someone we love is hurt? Is it wrong or negative to be jealous when someone betrays our love?

God Himself reveals anger, grief, and jealousy as well as love, joy, sorrow, and weariness. Emotions are part of being created in the image of God. They have much to teach us about life and relationship.

The following is a partial list of emotions. Even if you think of yourself as an unemotional person, I think you'll find that you have felt all of these emotions at one time or another. We all have that element in common: We feel.

What we do with the emotions can differ greatly, but the emotions themselves are part of what it means to be made in His likeness and to be human beings living in this world.

## A Partial List of Emotions
You can identify your emotions with two simple equations. Complete the sentences: "I feel_____" or "I am_____." This exercise helps to distinguish feelings from actions. The following fit into the equations quite easily:

| | | |
|---|---|---|
| loved | sad | insecure |
| unlovable | curious | afraid |
| joyful | elated | desperate |
| angry | disappointed | panicked |
| betrayed | jealous | nervous |
| depressed | understood | irresistible |
| happy | misunderstood | hungry |
| fulfilled | satisfied | brave |
| confused | blue | safe |
| weary | whole | excited |
| hurt | secure | old |
| left out | broken | complete |
| powerful | overpowered | weak |
| strong | bored | tense |
| surprised | admired | warm |
| patient | gentle | cherished |

There are many more emotions to add to the list. See how many you can come up with on your own.

Emotions aren't problematic when we allow ourselves to feel them and to identify the cause. They become a problem when we pretend they don't exist or try to deny their impact. The healthiest way to live is to be up to date with what we are feeling and what we are doing about those feelings.

## The Myth of "Weakness"

For many, expressing emotions is tantamount to admitting a weakness or need. After all, aren't we more powerful when people can't tell if we're bothered or hurt?

Sadly, many people hold to the above philosophy. Since they have been hurt or betrayed at some point in their lives, their logical solution is to keep people at arm's length, always unsure of what's going on inside. I understand. I too have been hurt beyond what I thought I was capable of handling.

We do get hurt in this world. And sometimes the exposure of our feelings and needs leads to being used by someone else. The answer isn't found in hiding who we are, it is in choosing well those we entrust with our hearts. It is also important to remember that even those we love most will hurt us from time to time.

We can trust people. We simply must trust them to be human—to hurt us at times and to disappoint. We all have that same inescapable problem: We cannot perfectly love.

Those who hurt are almost without question those who have been hurt through the years. They are the abused of yesterday who don't know how to fit their pain into today's relationships.

It is a myth that expressing emotions is equal to expressing weakness. I think our Lord showed this to be true better than anyone. He wept; He comforted; He asked for help; He grieved; He grew angry; He felt betrayed; and He very much wanted our love.

We do not see God as weak, but as a perfect balance of humility and strength, compassion and fortitude. He did not lose sight of His purpose, and neither did He lose sight of the needs of His people.

We can express emotions and still maintain our true strength. In fact, I believe only those who are comfortable with emotions are really strong. Strength isn't the absence of emotions, it is the honest and appropriate weaving together of those emotions into the fiber of our relationships. Where better to see such honesty modeled than in the church?

### The Myth of "Explosion"

There are some who are convinced that the next step in expressing emotions is losing control. And so they do. The problem, however, isn't in expressing emotions, it is in keeping them in for so long that, when finally let out, they become a nightmare. I understand the hesitation.

When we hold in our emotions, they build up just like steam in a pressure cooker. Then, when we least desire, those emotions come out in words or attitudes that we later regret.

Learn to express the emotions as they come. Express them at the appropriate time to the appropriate person, and they will lose their negative punch.

To withhold how we feel is not to protect, it is to model dishonesty and allow others to do the same. Emotions themselves do not explode on impact. How we live with those emotions is the key.

There is a simple way to help think through the feelings of the day. Ask yourself a few questions:

- "What are some of the emotions I experienced today?"
- "What did I do when I felt those emotions?"
- "What could I have done to deal with those emotions in a more honest, up-to-date way?"

The object of the exercise isn't necessarily to change your responses, but to make you aware of the emotions that are part of being you.

### The Myth of Protecting the Ones We Love

I see this myth lived out each time I enter the sanctuary of a family facing the terminal illness of one of its members. I can literally feel the feelings alive in the room, but no one is talking about them. One by one, all of the family members will tell me that they're just trying to *protect* the others by keeping the feelings within.

Believe it or not, when we withhold our feelings from one another, we leave everyone involved wondering about what's really going on. Sadly, left to our own devices, we generally draw faulty conclusions about one another's thoughts and needs. In time of trauma, we need to talk to one another more than any other time.

The same silence occurs in hospital rooms, in the wake of dissolved marriages, in the face of most other painful experiences. In the name of protecting one another, we generally rob one another of the joy of shared emotions and support.

If the goal were "being strong and hiding the hurts," why in the world did Jesus model such a lifestyle of sharing? Why did He invite the most loved disciples to accompany Him in His final moments of prayer? Why did He cry with Mary instead of just healing Lazarus in the first place?

There is no comfort in hidden emotions. There is only comfort in sharing with one another the various feelings, hurts, and needs that characterize our lives.

The best way to converse with a dying person is simply to say how you feel: "I hate to see you hurting this way." "I wish there were something I could do." "I'm going to miss you so much." "I'm afraid of going through this myself one day." "I feel so helpless." "Yesterday, I didn't come by because I was afraid to see you in pain."

The best way to converse with your children when the family is in pain is simply to say how you feel: "I'm sad today, honey, because I know I'm going to miss your mom." "I'm feeling a bit angry with God today. I know He has a purpose, but I'm hurting. You want to say a prayer with me?" "I bet you must be hurting too, because I am. It's OK to cry."

Nowhere else in the world can people experience the honesty of who they are better than in the midst of the body of believers. The church needn't fear the expression of emotions; feelings are part of our glorious heritage.

Can you imagine not having any feelings? Not hurting when someone else hurts or not feeling anger when someone is wronged? Emotions are a gift of God to be relished, understood, shared, and expressed. There is nothing brave about concealing how we feel.

# EIGHT

## A Closer Look at Grief

When we deal with suffering, whether physical, mental, or emotional, grief is part of the process. Often characterized as a "negative" emotion, grief carries a sense of embarrassment or frustration, as if we should somehow be able to handle our problems. In reality, we are simply afraid of grief because we don't know what to do or say to make it better.

It is easiest to understand grief as an emotional response to a painful event. When a relative dies, when a child leaves home, when a marriage dissolves, when we lose a job or change our employment, when we make a physical move, when we feel betrayed, when we've tried and tried but seem to go nowhere, when we go through certain stages of life, or when an illness is discovered in our bodies, we go through a natural process of grieving.

Grief is an emotional response to a painful event in our lives. There is no quick way to walk through the grieving process. For some it takes weeks; for some, months; for some, grief is expressed on and off for years. There is no magic time frame for dealing with grief, and no "more spiritual" way to handle the emotion.

### God's Grief: An Expression of Pain

Grief is a companion to suffering—and a very important one, even for God. I'll never forget the first time I really looked at the words in Genesis 6. The world as it had been created was lost.

Sin had entered in and, with it, the painful reminders of destruction. Imagine God's sorrow as He gazed upon the once "good" creation and saw it marred by sin. Come close to the heart of God's pain:

> The Lord saw how great man's wickedness on earth had become, and that every inclination of the thoughts of his heart was only evil all the time. The Lord was grieved that He had made man on the earth, and His heart was filled with pain (Gen. 6:5-6).

Can you imagine God grieving? Perhaps all of heaven stood still for a moment to give Him free reign with His pain. God grieved, and in His grief there was no solace. The reality was simple: Sin had brutally infected the ones He had created in His image.

## The Final Days of Our Lord

We also see grief expressed in the life of our Lord. At several points in His ministry He grieved with those who were suffering (the widow of Nain in Luke 7:11-17 and Martha and Mary in John 11). Then, in His final days, He grieved for Himself and His upcoming pain:

> He withdrew about a stone's throw beyond them, knelt down and prayed, "Father, if You are willing, take this cup from Me; yet not My will, but Yours be done." An angel from heaven appeared to Him and strengthened Him. And being in anguish, He prayed more earnestly, and His sweat was like drops of blood falling to the ground (Luke 22:41-44).

Our Lord was approaching death—not just physical death, but death of a kind you and I will never know. He bore on His shoulders the weight of sin, and that weight was far heavier than anyone can imagine.

> He grew up before Him like a tender shoot, and like a root out of dry ground. He had no beauty or majesty to attract us to Him, nothing in His appearance that

we should desire Him. He was despised and rejected by men, a man of sorrows, and familiar with suffering. Like one from whom men hide their faces He was despised, and we esteemed Him not. Surely He took up our infirmities and carried our sorrows, yet we considered Him stricken by God, smitten by Him, and afflicted. But He was pierced for our transgressions, He was crushed for our iniquities; the punishment that brought us peace was upon Him, and by His wounds we are healed. We all, like sheep, have gone astray, each of us has turned to his own way; and the Lord has laid on Him the iniquity of us all (Isa. 53:2-6).

Jesus suffered and grieved so much that even the comfort of His friends could not soften the blow. We don't look to our Lord and say, "Why should He have grieved?" We look to Him now and share in His grief.

### Shared Grief

Grieving isn't reserved for God. It is an emotion we share with God as we live out our lives in this world.

Grief is a natural response to suffering and the realities of sin and pain. It is an emotional gift from God to help us adjust and respond to the losses of this life. When we begin to accept that suffering is part of living here, then we begin to see that grieving is also an important part of the process. Join me in a closer look at grief.

### The Naked Reality of Sin

King David, God's servant, understood the grieving process well. Late in the prime of his life, David sent his warriors off to battle while he remained at home. We can only surmise as to why.

Perhaps he was tired of battling. Perhaps he was working through his own aging. Perhaps he was weary from his responsibilities as king. For a myriad of reasons, David did not accompany his troops, and a web of deceit followed.

The king was restless one evening and went for a walk on the roof. There he discovered a beautiful woman bathing.

Some think the encounter was by chance; some think Bathsheba planned the temptation. Whatever the circumstances, David watched for a time, probably argued with himself over the temptation of lust, and then allowed sin to work within him. The result of his evening stroll? An adulterous relationship with another man's wife, resulting in pregnancy.

At that point, David had a number of options. He could do the "godly" thing and reveal his sin, begging the forgiveness of Uriah, Bathsheba's husband. He could lie about the liaison altogether and leave Bathsheba to create another tale. He could bribe her to say the baby had been conceived during the last visit with her husband. Or he could devise another scheme. He chose the latter option.

Be honest for a moment. Haven't you experienced those times when, confronted with the effects of your own sin, you created a hundred scenarios to cover the truth? We all want to run when our sin nature becomes evident and threatens to expose us for who we are.

David chose to cover up his sinful liaison and end his embarrassment by planning Uriah's death in battle. The scheme worked, so to speak, but David's soul had no rest. Finally, after a humiliating encounter with Nathan, the prophet, David poured out his heart to God.

David grieved over his sin, and the grief was raw and bitter. He mourned, fasted, and prayed, but the child born from the sinful relationship fell ill and died. David tasted the grief of sin, and that grief remained part of his life for the remainder of his days (2 Sam. 11–12).

> Have mercy on me, O God, according to Your unfailing love; according to Your great compassion blot out my transgressions. Wash away all my iniquity and cleanse me from my sin. For I know my transgressions, and my sin is always before me. Against You, You only have I sinned and done what is evil in Your sight, so that You are proved right when You speak and justified when You judge. Surely I have been sinful from birth, sinful from the time my mother conceived me. Surely You desire truth in the inner parts; You teach me wisdom in the inmost place. Cleanse me with hyssop, and I will be clean; wash

me, and I will be whiter than snow. Let me hear joy
and gladness; let the bones You have crushed rejoice.
Hide Your face from my sins and blot out all my
iniquity. Create in me a pure heart, O God, and
renew a steadfast spirit within me. Do not cast me
from Your presence or take Your Holy Spirit from
me. Restore to me the joy of Your salvation and grant
me a willing spirit, to sustain me (Ps. 51:1-12).

The grief from our sins is real. It is only when we run from
reality that sin doesn't seem to matter. When finally we stop
running, the hurt is still there, and it is an important part of the
healing.

David was well-acquainted with his own sinful nature. The
grief of introspection brought him closer to God and enabled
him to bear the pain of those he loved. He could comfort
Bathsheba with the comfort—as costly as it was—that he had
received from God (2 Sam. 12:24).

When we think of people in Scripture who suffered grief in
response to sin, we don't have to go very far. Adam and Eve
suffered the loss of their own wholeness and the effects that it
had on their children (Gen. 3–4). Noah grieved because the
effects of sin returned so quickly after the Flood (Gen. 7–9).

Abraham grieved over the greed that separated him from Lot
(Gen. 13) and over the jealousy that divided Sarah and Hagar
(Gen. 16 and 21). Jacob was filled with grief over the loss of his
beloved son, Joseph—only to grieve again years later upon dis-
covering the hatred that had driven his other sons to deeds of
lies and deception (Gen. 37–50).

The results of sin are companions to grief. Should we have
any other response? Isn't it natural, even godly, to grieve when
faced with the realities of sin in our lives? I believe so. I believe
we share this powerful emotion with a loving God who, Himself,
grieves deeply over the destructive nature of sin.

### The Deep Pain of Loss
Not only is grief a companion to sin, it is a friend to loss.
Grieving is a way that you and I can express our hurt over losing
someone or something that has played an important role in our
lives.

David knew about loss. While young, he was invited into Saul's household. Saul loved to hear David play his music (1 Sam. 16:14-23) and David enjoyed serving the king.

Problems arose, however, as David matured and began to assume leadership in Israel. Saul didn't mind David's personal service, but he was jealous of David's growing influence in God's kingdom. Though God officially removed Saul from the throne, Saul wasn't willing to step down.

Saul's jealousy grew with each passing day, until he placed himself literally at war with young David. David had every reason to despise Saul, but such was not in David's nature. David loved Saul and Saul's son, Jonathan (18:1-4; 20), and David grieved deeply over the pain in their relationships.

Tragically, in the heat of one of the battles, Saul and Jonathan finally met their death. The loss of those two grieved David's heart deeply. He also grieved because of the pain he felt whenever he remembered their lives and their deaths. He grieved because a part of himself had died too. When we lose someone we love, the heart bears a heavy weight. Listen to David's lament over the loss of his beloved friends.

> Saul and Jonathan — in life they were loved and gracious, and in death they were not parted. They were swifter than eagles, they were stronger than lions. O daughters of Israel, weep for Saul, who clothed you in scarlet and finery, who adorned your garments with ornaments of gold. How the mighty have fallen in battle! Jonathan lies slain on your heights. I grieve for you, Jonathan my brother; you were very dear to me. Your love for me was wonderful, more wonderful than that of women (2 Sam. 1:23-26).

Elisha also knew the pain of losing someone he loved. His story reveals a man who is similar to many of us, both in his dedication to a friend and avoidance of pain.

The time had come for Elijah the prophet to be taken up to meet God. Elisha felt very close to Elijah, and though Elisha knew the time was ripe, he didn't want to discuss his loss.

The company of the prophets at Bethel came out to

Elisha and asked, "Do you know that the Lord is going to take your master from you today?"

"Yes, I know," Elisha replied, "but do not speak of it."

Then Elijah said to him, "Stay here, Elisha, the Lord has sent me to Jericho."

And he replied, "As surely as the Lord lives and as you live, I will not leave you." So they went to Jericho (2 Kings 2:3-4).

The same basic conversation was exchanged another time until the Lord did, indeed, take Elijah up into heaven in a whirlwind. Elisha wanted to hold onto his master as long as possible. He loved Elijah and didn't want to think of God taking him away.

The prophet grieved as well. He tried to protect Elisha from the pain of his departure, but Elisha would not listen. He wanted only to accompany his master to the end. The friendship they shared was that deep.

When we are forced to say "good-bye" to someone we love, we grieve. There is nothing shameful or weak about the grief, it is part of the beauty of loving someone.

Even though we know that life does not stand still and protect those relationships that are sacred to us, we cannot help but experience sorrow when the time of the loss is upon us.

### Common Experiences of Grief

In recent years, studies have been done that assign numerical value to the elements of stress in our lives. The idea is to *rate* your stress level based on the experiences you've endured.

Rated high on the scale are many situations which result in expressions of grief. As caregivers, we need to pay close attention to common causes of such sadness.

The following are in no particular order of significance. Keep in mind that even though some of these stressful experiences are also desirable ones, they are emotionally costly just the same.

*Experiences and Grief: Common Companions*

| | |
|---|---|
| Death of a spouse | Death of a child |
| Death of a parent | Divorce |

70

A physical move
Incarceration
Birth of a child
Promotion
Adolescence
Legal encounter
Financial strains
Aging of parents
Placing a parent in a care facility
Long hours of work
Moving of a close friend
Weight gain or loss

Traumatic illness
Marriage
Fire, flood, earthquake
Undesired change in job
Accident
Bankruptcy
War
Rape, incest, abuse
Prolonged hospitalization
Return to school
Alcohol or drug abuse
Aging

As you can see, the life experiences that produce stress generally produce grief as well — and the above is just a partial list.

A change in pastoral leadership at the church can produce grief. The loss of favor with a close friend can really hurt. There are many scenarios that face us all, and they need the attention of the church. We need to have a place to go where grief is understood and shared.

## Common Expressions of Grief

Though the following expressions are not all-inclusive, they do give us a fairly good place to start. People who are grieving will generally exhibit one or more of the following signs. In other words, they need our help and support.

Observe the possible symptoms of grief and write them on your heart. Be ready and willing to reach out when there is someone who needs your love.

*Common Expressions of Grief*

- Loss of appetite
- Excessive, almost mindless eating
- Disbelief/shock (failure to accept the reality of the loss)
- Nervous behaviors (nonstop cleaning, biting of nails, compulsive need to work, excessive use of television, etc.)
- Sexual disinterest or dysfunctions

71

- Inability to make decisions
- Anger (turned inward or outward)
- Trouble maintaining close relationships
- Lethargy
- Short attention span
- Seeming loss of short-term memory
- Lack of interest in spiritual things
- Increased, almost obsessive interest in spiritual things
- Need to keep talking about the loss, even when another conversation is taking place
- Flow of tears or seeming absence of tears
- Disinterest in activity, even with old friends or family
- Lack of concern for good eating and sleeping habits
- Periods of staring off "into space"
- Waking in the middle of the night

Some people handle their grief almost naturally. They are generally those who have had good models in the past in dealing with emotions and expressing needs. For those people, the days of grief will be real, but their interaction with others and with life will be almost uninterrupted. It is these people we usually feel most comfortable with in their grief. It is these people that we say handle their grief well.

Others have more difficulty handling their pain, and they need not be feared or avoided. Such people need the help of the church more than ever. They need friends who will stand by them, even though it's costly and, at times, uncomfortable.

Please keep in mind that grieving is a natural process. It is a privilege that goes along with loving. Were we able to just "live and let live," we, of all people, would be most deserving of pity.

The fact that our God loves so deeply means that He, and we in His image, also hurt deeply. Joy and grief are opposite sides of the same, cherished coin.

# NINE

## A Closer Look
## at Depression

As we have looked at grief, we have seen that it is generally associated with a loss. Sometimes the loss is a physical one; sometimes it is more the loss of an ideal or a dream. Neither are difficult to imagine. When we suffer a loss, we hurt.

Depression falls close on the heels of grief. While grief is generally associated with a specific event, depression is usually initiated by a loss but representative of much more. To put it simply, depression generally represents a number of perceived or real losses, all rolled into one, dark feeling.

I would like to differentiate here between clinical depression and depression that is felt by a number of men, women, and children in our world today. Clinical depression is often treated best with a combination of psychological and medical therapy. It is described, in laymen's terms, as a chemical imbalance in the body, brought on by a number of possible combinations.

It is not necessary for me to address the therapy involved with clinical depression since such a diagnosis is individual and best discussed between patient and physician. (For a list of books on depression, see Appendix B.) What we will discuss here should be of benefit to the clinically depressed, as well as to all who want to help those who are suffering from depression.

### A World of Darkness

Most people who have been depressed at some point in time describe the depression as a great darkness. Not only does the person grieve, but the grief feels like a prolonged death—a black hole, a dark night. Unfortunately, people often seem lost in this dark night because they feel alone or, in the case of believers, ashamed. Somehow, they've been taught they shouldn't feel depressed. Yet the emotions live on.

Is it wrong for the believer to be depressed? Can't a person of faith draw on God and His Word to end this dark feeling? Should anything upset the Christian to the point of depression? What leads to depression, and how can it be controlled?

The answers are neither simple nor are they always the same for everyone. Darkness to one may seem insignificant to another, which is what makes ministry to those who are depressed so delicate. We need to be sensitive, to listen, to observe, to share, to ask questions, to accept the silence and the tears.

### The Pain of Letting Go

At the risk of oversimplifying the process, try to think of depression as the feeling that occurs when we must "let go," but we don't know how. The pain has come on too swiftly, and we're not sure how to get our lives back on track. Let me explain:

All of us have dreams, relationships, expectations, and belongings that we hold to and believe in. In fact, these dreams, relationships, expectations, and belongings form the basis for our lives. Take the following circle, for example—like pieces of a pie filled in to represent the interests of most people in this world.

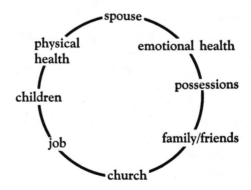

The above circle is generic in nature, but we could easily personalize the circle to reflect our own families, values, and goals. The contents of the circle are dear to us, and as long as we keep

74

the pie intact, all is basically well.

Now imagine a situation. John and Nancy Green have been married for thirteen years. They have three children, two boys and a girl. John has a good job as assistant manager in a growing firm. The entire family knows the Lord as Savior, and the church family is kind and supportive. In short, all has been going well—basically according to plan.

One day, John receives a call at work from his wife. It seems that the doctors, in a routine exam, found what they suspect to be leukemia in their smallest child's body. Their world begins to turn upside down.

Months pass. There are doctor's appointments, bills to pay, chemotherapy treatments, long hours to endure. They don't dare let themselves speak of death, but it doesn't look good. John wants to be more closely involved in the day-to-day activities, but he must retain his position at work, just to keep food on the table.

Friends helped at first, but everyone has returned to their own commitments and families. The Greens don't blame anyone, they just carry on. Both are losing weight. Both are emotionally and physically exhausted. Both feel helpless to remove this pain from the life of their little boy. Eighteen months later, the child's body succumbs to the disease.

Go back to the circle diagram for a moment. Do you see what has happened? Almost all of the pieces of the pie have been severely disturbed by the entrance of cancer. Where once their lives were steady, now they can't even remember how steady felt. So many of their securities have been wrenched from their grasp, yet how do they say "Good-bye"? Where do they begin to grieve?

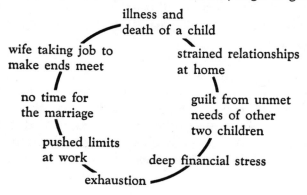

The Greens must turn loose of the pain and allow healing to come into their lives, if for no other reason, for the sake of the son and daughter still very much alive. But, as you can see, their grief is about much more than the loss of their child; it's about the complete disruption of their lives, their health, their family, their finances. Depression will certainly be part of the healing process.

Illness is not the only devastation accompanied by depression. I have worked with a number of men and women who, in their thirties, forties, or fifties, suddenly suffer depression. Many were the victims of sexual or physical abuse as children. Many are adult children of alcoholics.

Many have felt undeserving or inferior for years. Many are living a life much different than they had dreamed. Many have simply run out of energy in their escape from painful memories or disappointments.

It isn't that we know the pain is lurking underneath. In fact, sometimes the memories are deeply buried until something happens to call them to the surface once again. For a variety of reasons, depression sets in, and we struggle to find its origin before moving on. If the ingredients remain a mystery, the depression is likely to continue.

While it is difficult to turn loose and accept our losses, it is critical that we do so, if we are to grow from depression rather than wither from its strain. Accepting life's pains is a must for all of us, since life does offer pain.

Depression is an emotional response that can occur in anyone's life. It is neither a sin to struggle with depression, nor is it a sign of some weakness. Sometimes some of us struggle more deeply than we had ever thought possible. Sometimes we need help to walk out of the great darkness. God is not absent from depression; He is there.

### Cool Water, Hot Bread

Elijah was a prophet after God's own heart. He was strong, committed, brave, and compassionate—all the qualities we deem admirable in the life of a servant of God. He was also steadfast in his faith even when other prophets had been persecuted and killed. In short, Elijah was a courageous and purposed man of God.

The story most remember about Elijah springs from his encounter with the prophets of Baal on Mount Carmel. Elijah
alone represented God, while 450 prophets were there in the
name of Baal. The object was to see which god was the true
God. After many useless hours of empty prayers on the part of
the prophets of Baal, Elijah's God won (1 Kings 18).

We would think that such a victory would leave Elijah elated,
and I imagine that he was. But often, in the wake of victory lies
a certain weariness from the battle. Elijah met that weariness
head on.

Jezebel, a wicked woman who hated to lose, was furious when
she discovered Elijah's celebration. She sent a note warning him
that his death was near (19:2). After all that Elijah had just
experienced, he could easily have laughed in the face of her
threats. Instead, the prophet "ran for his life" through Judah and
into a lonely, dry desert (vv. 3-4).

" 'I have had enough, Lord,' he said. 'Take my life; I am no
better than my ancestors.' Then he lay down under the tree and
fell asleep" (vv. 4-5a).

Why should the prophet feel depressed? Why should he want
to die? He had everything going for him, didn't he? What more
could he possibly want than to single-handedly defeat the false
prophets of Baal? Elijah had every reason to feel strong and
courageous after his victory; instead, he felt weak and lonely and
afraid.

God is kind to us when we are suffering. He sends comfort in
ways that are particular to our needs. The picture of God's
comfort for the weary prophet is an example of His unfailing
love.

> All at once, an angel touched him and said, "Get up
> and eat." He looked around, and there by his head
> was a cake of bread baked over hot coals, and a jar of
> water. He ate and drank and then lay down again.
> The angel of the Lord came back a second time and
> touched him and said, "Get up and eat, for the jour-
> ney is too much for you." So he got up and ate and
> drank. Strengthened by that food, he traveled forty
> days and forty nights until he reached Horeb, the
> mountain of God (vv. 5b-8).

God didn't chastise Elijah in his depression. He didn't lecture the prophet in the fine art of faith. He didn't blame Elijah for growing weary and afraid. After all, Elijah thought he was alone. Other prophets had been killed, and Jezebel was a wicked, formidable enemy. True, he had conquered the prophets of Baal, but that battle wasn't the end of the war. Elijah was tired of being alone. Can you imagine Elijah's surprise when he woke to the smell of fresh-baked bread? God could have sent the food precooked, but the prophet needed a personal touch. God's angel cooked for the prophet and ministered to him in a gentle, encouraging way.

The rest of the story is equally touching. The Lord told Elijah to stand and wait on the mountain for the Lord to pass by. Elijah obeyed.

A powerful wind tore the mountains apart, but God was not in the wind. An earthquake shook the ground where he stood, but the Lord was not in the earthquake. A fire swept the land round about him, but the Lord was not in the fire.

Then, Elijah heard Him. Yes, it was God. He passed in a gentle whisper, promising His own presence and the company of other men to serve alongside the prophet for the battles still to come (vv. 11-18). The war was not over, but neither was Elijah alone.

Elijah felt hopeless, purposeless, weary, parched—but God was there. His depression wasn't scolded or mocked, but met by the love of God.

### The Land of Deepest Night

Elijah wasn't the only servant of God to suffer depression. Job was well acquainted with the affliction. He had lost everything to Satan's ploys, and life itself was without meaning. Listen to the echoes of his pain:

> May the day of my birth perish, and the night it was said, "A boy is born!" That day—may it turn to darkness; may God above not care about it; may no light shine upon it (Job 3:3-4).

> If only my anguish could be weighed and all my misery be placed on the scales! It would surely outweigh

the sand of the seas—no wonder my words have been impetuous. The arrows of the Almighty are in me, my spirit drinks in their poison; God's terrors are marshaled against me. . . . Oh, that I might have my request, that God would grant what I hope for, that God would be willing to crush me, to let loose His hand and cut me off. . . . What strength do I have, that I should still hope? What prospects, that I should be patient? Do I have the strength of stone? Is my flesh bronze? Do I have any power to help myself, now that success has been driven from me? (6:2-4, 8-9, 11-13)

When I read that passage to clients or friends who suffer from depression, they say that Job grasps their pain. Depression carries a sort of hopelessness and darkness that can't quite be captured by words, but Job came awfully close.

God allowed Satan to destroy Job's world. The very things Job counted as important: his children, his animals, his servants, his friendships, his physical well-being—all were taken by the enemy. Job had little left to hold onto, and little to hope for . . . or so he thought.

Day after day he poured out his darkness to God. "Why am I here?" "Where are You?" "Why was I born?" "Nothing good can come out of this." "What have I done wrong?" "Do You find pleasure in my grief?" Questions and statements of hopeless despair fell from Job's mouth to God's ear. Finally, God answered.

As we have seen before, the revelation from God was neither a response to Job's questions nor a promise of restoration. Instead, God's response to Job was to show Himself in His splendor. He revealed Himself to Job as one worthy of trust and full of purpose.

God was sensitive, yet strong—kind, yet honest. He gave Job a perspective to last a lifetime and peace to pass all understanding. Before Job had tasted any relief, his own words describe the gift of comfort God gave him:

Surely I spoke of things I did not understand, things too wonderful for me to know. . . . My ears had heard of You, but now my eyes have seen You (42:3, 5).

Again, no punishment for the depression; instead, a new way of seeing God, life, and self. What more do we need?

**Common Experiences of Depression**
Like grief, depression shares common experiences of change, loss, hurt. With depression, however, there are generally several factors of loss working together at the same time to sear the grief deep into our hearts and minds. The following list is only partial:

*Experiences of Depression*

| | |
|---|---|
| Death of a spouse | Death of a child |
| Death of a parent | Illness of a child |
| Illness of a spouse | Illness of a parent |
| Death or illness of a friend | Move of a friend |
| Physical move on our part | Divorce |
| Fire, flood, earthquake | Deep disappointment |
| Loss of faculty or limb | Loss of a dream or goal |
| Aging | Bankruptcy |

Unwanted change in employment or responsibility
Traumatic event, such as rape, incest, physical abuse, neglect
Being passed over for a certain job or promotion
Past experiences rising to the surface
Trying to live up to someone else's expectations
Trying to "perfectly" handle an imperfect world

**Common Expressions of Depression**
Like grief, the expressions of depression are generally found in the following list; though, again, this list is partial. Often more than one description fits, and sometimes the symptoms change from day-to-day.

*Common Expressions of Depression*

- Crying
- Loss of appetite
- Severe weight gain or fluctuation
- Extreme or constant fatigue
- Anger

- Apathy
- Lack of motivation
- Overreaction (a "short fuse" or ready supply of tears)
- Short to no attention span
- Loss of short-term memory/forgetfulness
- Lack of concern for personal well-being—physical, mental, and emotional
- Withdrawal into self
- Little to no interest in outside activities or friendships
- Sexual disinterest or dysfunction
- Compulsive behaviors: work, eating, activity, cleaning, etc.
- Sense of doom
- Desire to "stay in bed" or otherwise remain inactive
- Inability to remember yesterday's joys
- Inability to imagine tomorrow's joys and purpose
- Inability to make decisions
- Feelings of guilt and failed responsibilities

### Seeing Ourselves in the Mirror

Depression is not a pleasant emotional package. In fact, the unpleasant feelings are precisely the reason people who are depressed for very long give up. They cannot see a conclusion to their pain; so they want to be left alone until some end comes.

Fortunately, depression rarely kills us, and God *can* provide comfort, purpose, and true hope to the depressed. As we saw in the cases of Elijah and Job, the sun does rise again, and its light forces the darkness back into its place. It is important that we hold on and allow God to minister through His love and the love of His people.

A great gift of depression is that it provides us with an opportunity for self-evaluation and cleansing, of a sort. If no bruises appeared, we wouldn't know we had been internally hurt. The same is true for depression.

Depression is a sign that something is hurting deep inside which needs our undivided attention. Try to identify the sources of the pain—the pieces of the pie that are suffering a loss. Such identification is a place to begin seeing ourselves in the mirror of God's healing.

# TEN

## Comforting Those Who Suffer

Perhaps one of the most important comforts of the church lies in its ministry to those who are grieving and suffering from depression. Why? Simply because grief and depression touch so many lives as a result of so many different hurts.

From chronic illness or death to uncontrolled anger or the use of alcohol, grief and depression mark the pain. Comfort lies in the hands of those who reach out at such critical moments.

There are those who say, "But I don't understand the problem" or "I've never been through that myself, so how can I help?" Those are legitimate concerns, but the fact of the matter is we have all struggled from time to time, and our struggle speaks a universal language. Like a cool spring on a hot day, the comfort of a friend soothes the wound.

### Recognizing the Need
I think one of the most thoughtful steps in comforting someone comes in the very first moments of encounter. When you step into the room, making eye contact and sizing up the pain, it is a sensitive time.

Jesus seemed to be very good at first moments. He knew right away whether the person needed a helping hand, a gentle touch, a reminder of significance, a chance to be responsible, a strong "kick in the pants," a rebuke, or simply the freedom to share tears. All of the above are forms of comfort, and people need different things at different times. Let me illustrate.

A young, adolescent girl comes home in tears because her boyfriend just broke up with her. She needs safe arms and understanding. She has the right, so to speak, to be in a not-so-good mood for a while. She's been hurt.

The same young woman, a month later, doesn't need a free leash to treat other members of the family harshly or disrespectfully. At this point in the process, she needs some well-chosen words, spoken with equal kindness and to remind her of her responsibilities. She needs to begin to work through the hurt feelings.

A father of two small children has been laid off of his job at a large manufacturing company. He is given severance pay and a recommendation, but no one seems to be hiring in his area.

No one begrudges the man some moments of grief after losing his job. If he begins to stay at home and watch television day in and day out, however, someone needs to intervene.

The man is grieving. He has lost his livelihood, but, even more significant, his pride. He believes the husband and father should take care of the family, and he can't do that now. He needs a new vision; someone to help him with ideas; someone to encourage him and help him see his strengths and abilities.

An older man and woman have just started their years of retirement when the man suffers a severe heart attack and, subsequently, undergoes open-heart surgery. They had planned to travel and enjoy their retirement years, but now he is afraid to stray too far from home.

He knows he is disappointing his wife, but he doesn't know how to beat the fear. She is angry at the change in lifestyle but feels guilty for the anger.

He needs to talk about his fears, including his fear of death. Almost all heart patients experience such fear, but they don't know how to talk about it with their loved ones.

She needs to talk about her anger and not protect her husband from the feelings. They need a friend to help them talk together and listen to each other. The communication is essential to their learning how to support each other again.

### Helpful Ways to Offer Comfort
*Acceptance.* By far the most important need of anyone who is grieving lies in the acceptance of family members and friends.

83

Often the grieving feel guilty, ashamed. Often they feel as if no one understands, as if they're burdening others with their pain.

Let your comfort begin with acceptance. Gently remind the person that you're there, and that you want to understand his or her feelings. Acceptance takes a great load off the person.

*Listening.* I often wonder how many people feel "heard" in this world. Think just about family life alone. When everyone is seated at the table for a meal, silence is not usually the term that describes the interaction.

We want to be heard, so the race is on for the attention of mom, dad, husband, or wife. At times we finish one another's sentences. At times we're off in another world while someone is sharing a story. At times we're too busy or tired to listen.

Take time to listen. A grieving person really longs to be heard. Resist the temptation to give advice, to fill in gaps, to complete sentences. Just be there and listen.

*Touch.* As we mentioned earlier in this book, touch is a marvelous way of saying, "I love you, and I understand." When we're grieving, we feel alone, but touch brings concern. What is it about touch? It only takes a moment. It is a posture, an attitude. It is reaching out with a gift that bridges hearts.

*Identify the Loss.* This part of comfort takes a little work and some time to think. When we grieve and, particularly, when depression sets in, the first steps on the road to recovery are found in identifying the elements of our loss.

You might simply draw a circle for the person, dividing it into parts and writing in the losses. The following serves as an example for the older couple facing retirement and heart disease:

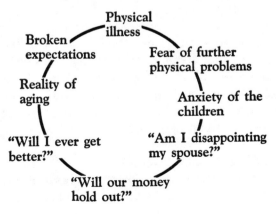

Physical illness

Broken expectations

Fear of further physical problems

Reality of aging

Anxiety of the children

"Will I ever get better?"

"Am I disappointing my spouse?"

"Will our money hold out?"

When the above elements are seen, it makes the grief or depression a little more manageable. We can see the hurt, the questions, and the fears, and we can accept or resolve them one by one.

The process of identifying the loss is not a difficult one, unless there are secrets beneath the surface that haven't been viewed for years. In such case, you may need the insight of your pastor or a professional counselor to help unearth the pain and deal with it in a healthy manner.

How will you know if something lurks beneath the surface? Generally, if talking, listening, touching, and identifying the losses don't help, there is a more serious problem.

If the tears persist and the hopelessness continues, seek the advice of someone who has dealt with grief and depression professionally. Stay with the person you're comforting, and simply suggest that you will call in someone else for support.

Please remember to remain a part of the process, even if professional counseling or a treatment facility is necessary. As a person of comfort, you play a big role in the healing.

*An Atmosphere of Openness.* Most of us make the mistake of treating suffering in hushed tones. We talk about anything else but "it." An important step in bringing comfort to those who are grieving lies in helping the family and friends to be open about the process.

Family members and friends need to know that it's not only "OK" but also very healthy for the grieving person to verbalize his or her feelings. The reverse side of the coin is also true. Loved ones need to verbalize their grief, anger, or frustration so that months of emotions don't get bottled up inside.

Is it all right for a family member to need space? Absolutely. Should that person pretend they have some previous engagement? No. Help the family members and friends learn to talk to one another.

John: "Mom, I know that you're hurting, and I want to be here for you, but right now I just need some space."

Mom: "I understand, honey. You're helping me by listening, and I can certainly help you by giving you space."

85

I don't in any way want to oversimplify the process, but communication really can be rather simple. What often occurs is the hiding of feelings rather than their disclosure. We try to protect one another; we assume others don't care; and before we know it, we've forgotten how to simply say what we feel and what we need.

Take a lesson here from little children. When they don't like something you put in their mouths, they spit it out. When they don't understand, they ask again. When they're bored, they fall asleep or otherwise occupy the time. When they're hurt, they cry. When they're content, they cuddle and laugh.

Children don't learn until later how to hide what they like or dislike, feel, or think. In times of grieving or depression, we need to return to simple openness.

I am not advising that all members of the family say everything that comes to mind. That kind of openness is rarely appropriate in any situation. What I'm saying is that honesty needs to be preserved, encouraged, and modeled in times of grief.

If a young mother dies from illness or accident, her children need to talk about their fears, hurts, and needs. If a father is ill and not doing well, his family needs to share those moments together.

I have known a family who did this very well. The father and beloved husband was ill from cancer of the brain. Two little children faced the loss of someone very important to their lives. A young wife faced months of taking care of the one who used to take care of her. At the end, she changed his diapers and fed him, just as the two of them had done together for their children.

They made it through by being open with one another. The children asked questions; they all cried; death was discussed time and again; they prayed together. They walked through the grief one day at a time, hand in hand with one another.

Help those who are hurting do the same.

*Recording the Feelings and the Growth.* Some people are at home with a pen and a notebook. Some are not. Some people find it easy to express themselves. Some have never really tried.

One sure way to get the comfort flowing from the inside out is to encourage those who are grieving to write down their thoughts and feelings, questions and fears. The writing opens up what's inside and helps the person to face the process. It is an excellent tool of comfort.

Audio recordings can be another means of recording the days. For some, talking into the tape collects the thoughts and places them in some organized form. It also becomes a record, as does the writing, of all that has transpired—a record that will prove a godsend in years to come.

*Prayer.* Though prayer is often misused, it is certainly a gift of comfort. Generally, a friend or an elder comes to call from the church and begins or ends with a prayer. That alone can lift the sense of burden.

There is, however, another important gift that prayer brings to the grieving. It gives those who are hurting opportunity to voice their needs to the One whose love is unfailing. Even if the grieving person is angry with God, prayer gets the feelings flowing upward and not just inward.

Remember the unfolding of Job's grief and depression. He started out the process talking with God. In fact, we're told that Job, upon losing his children, his servants, his livestock, and his dreams, tore his robes and prayed to God these incredible words of humility:

> Naked I came from my mother's womb, and naked I will depart. The Lord gave and the Lord has taken away; may the name of the Lord be praised (Job 1:21).

The words almost seem too good to be true, but Job was a man who loved God. In the face of such incredible loss, he turned to the only One he knew who could give comfort.

Job's grief had just begun, however. His physical health was taken away. Job's wife encouraged him to curse God and die. His friends began to link his loss with some sin he must have committed. And before he knew what was happening, the happy life Job had known was destroyed.

The first nine chapters are filled with Job's complaints and questions for God. In what seems like an almost continual debate with his friends, Job tried to analyze God's purposes and redefine his own importance. Job did quite a bit of talking *about* God in those days, but very little talking *with* God.

Most grieving people pattern their thoughts and conversations after Job's. They spend hours trying to figure out the whys and wherefores of their pain. They talk about God and think about their anger or hurt, but they spend little time directly talking with Him. This is where the well-placed prayers of a comfort-bearer come in.

Help the person learn to talk with God about the questions and the pain. He doesn't mind the anger or the hurt. Once Job's prayers were turned upward, little by little he began to discover a perspective that had eluded him in his pain.

Praying *for* someone is a wonderful gift. Praying *with* someone — even if that person chooses to remain silent — encourages the floodgates to be opened outward and upward. Praying *with* encourages the relationship with God to continue, no matter how hurt, angry, or awkward. God doesn't mind the strain. He longs to be invited into the grief.

*Responsibility.* We come, again, to this very important aspect of comfort. And, once more, I remind you that it's often the most difficult aspect for us to include in our caregiving. It is hard to know when to push the sufferer into responsibility.

People who are grieving or depressed often lose interest in aspects of life that are significant to everyone else. Food, sleep, work, a clean house, exercise, relationships, emotional well-being seem to be down the list of importance.

Comforting someone who grieves for a prolonged period of time involves helping that person take responsibility again. It involves bringing that person back down to earth where life is still being lived and where people are still depending on one another to carry a measure of the burden.

I have seen many men and women pull out of their friendships and activities, all in the very appropriate name of needing a bit of space to re-collect perspective. Such a vacation from life is necessary. But vacations don't last forever! In fact, the longer we allow the rest from responsibilities to last, the harder it is to get going again.

You might literally help a person dress and take that person on a walk around the block. You might literally take food and watch while the grieving one eats. You might insist on taking the person out for a while. You might insist on helping that person get back into the mainstream of life.

Why is this important? Because we are part of this life until the Lord chooses to take us home; and as long as we are here, there is work to be done. People need us; we need them. Even the mundane activities of life are necessary.

Simply put, when we avoid the sunlight for too long, it hurts our eyes and obscures our vision. Grief and depression are normal parts of this world's process, but they become unhealthy aspects if life stops there.

The person may not be too fond of you at the moment of intervention, but later that person will be grateful that you cared enough to help him or her become responsible again.

In summary, there is a season simply to hold and listen. But there is also a season for responsibility. Here are some of the important routines to encourage those who are suffering to become responsible:

- Sleep and rest
- Good eating habits
- Physical exercise
- A "normal" schedule
- Work of some kind
- Involvement in family activities
- Involvement in church activities
- Going through the reminders (for example, going through the belongings of a loved one who died)

*Songs of Comfort.* Most of us know just how on target Scripture can be in our lives. How many times have you opened the Word, only to find a message of encouragement that was needed right then? God left us with a storehouse of wisdom and guidance, and that storehouse includes songs of comfort.

A marvelous gift of comfort comes through the psalms of David, Asaph, and others. The psalms are some of the most emotionally revealing words found in the Bible. They reflect the fears, the angers, the weariness, the needs, the bitterness, the memories, the agony, and the joys of God's beloved servants. They were written long ago, but they could have been written yesterday by those of us who have suffered grief.

You might simply introduce the grieving person to the songs of comfort. Some of the psalms may seem depressing to those who are feeling well at the moment, but the candor is so refreshing to those who are suffering. It seems that the writers literally know the heart and thoughts of those who feel depressed. Such songs bring much comfort to the sorrowful.

Particular psalms of comfort include Psalms 3, 5–7, 9–13, 16, 18, 22–23, 28, 30–31, 34–35, 38, 40 . . . And the list goes on!

Read the psalms and allow them entrance into your own heart. Then they will become tools for your caregiving—comforts for the pain and grief for the people you love.

*The Importance of Regaining Perspective.* One of the most telltale signs of Job's depression can be found in the words of his journal. Remember the despair when he said:

> Why then did You bring me out of the womb? I wish I had died before any eye saw me. If only I had never come into being, or had been carried straight from the womb to the grave! Are not my few days almost over? Turn away from me so I can have a moment's joy before I go to the place of no return, to the land of gloom and deep shadow, to the land of deepest night, of deep shadow and disorder, where even the light is like darkness (Job 10:18-22).

Those words reveal Job's loss of perspective. He couldn't remember yesterday's accomplishments and joys, and he couldn't imagine tomorrow's peace. Lost in such turmoil, Job felt he had no purpose to live.

As a bearer of comfort, help the grieving one gain perspective once again. Life has had meaning and will have meaning once more. There have been joys, and there will be joys again.

It is difficult to remember the healthiness of the past when the present feels so devastating. And it is difficult to imagine a healthy tomorrow when we can't get past today.

There have been losses. There will always be losses—just as there have been and will always be gains. All of the ingredients come together to make up our experience in this world.

*Coming to Terms with the Loss.* I left this part of comfort for last because it's the underlying necessity in the healing process of the one who grieves. We have discussed the importance of identifying the loss, but coming to terms requires more time, more energy, and more courage than does the identification.

Depression grows deep when we refuse to turn loose. The more we refuse, the darker the night closes in around us.

Life is hard. Jesus warned us that life would be hard. No place in the Scripture are we fooled into thinking that this world will be a pleasant place filled only with pleasant things. Since all must endure hardship and loss, we must come to terms with that loss if we are to experience health and another beginning.

When I work with people who are suffering from depression, I usually ask them to help me complete a simple equation about their lives. I ask them to tell what their "givens" are at the moment—those things about their lives that are not likely to change anytime soon. Let me explain.

My "givens" are that I am single. I am a woman. I have struggled with cancer for some time. I live daily with physical pain. I have bills to take care of, a home to keep clean, and a body to feed and clothe. I get lonely at times. I travel quite a bit and speak, which means I step in and out of peoples' lives, and I miss them when I'm gone. I have a mother, father, sister, brother-in-law, and three nieces (beautiful, I might add!). The list goes on.

Most of what we fight against are our "givens." Some people's lists include divorce, loss of husband or wife to illness or accident, chronic illness in the family, weight problems, eating disorders, alcohol problems, loss of job, change of address or direction, and so on.

The very things that usually cause prolonged depression are circumstances we can do little or nothing about. When that becomes clear, we feel hopeless, helpless, angry, or confused.

We cannot change many of life's circumstances. What we can change is how we view those circumstances and how we allow them to affect our lives. I cannot change the reality of my pain, so I have learned to grow with that pain and see it as a sort of companion. Changing my thinking has made a world of difference.

I used to be awakened by pain in the wee hours of the morning. I felt sorry for myself and angry with God and the world for the affliction that cost me sleep and comfort. I was only twenty-eight at the outset of my experience with cancer, and I couldn't believe God expected me to live with pain for years on end.

I now see the pain through different eyes. Since I have accepted the part it plays in my life, I try to see my circumstance through eyes of belief rather than disbelief. I suppose you could say that I have learned to trust God in a way I never had before.

Accepting the loss doesn't mean forgetting the loss or pretending it doesn't hurt. It simply means starting over with a new "normal." One of the great blessings of grace for the believer lies in the fact that we don't need to return to normal to receive comfort. We have the privilege of heading into a new "normal," with the strength of God on our side.

I know there are those who say that suffering need not exist in our lives, but I can tell you that few words bring less comfort to the grieving than words spoken through a "God doesn't want you to suffer" perspective. People who are grieving or suffering from depression are well aware of the reality of pain.

Accepting the loss means taking a look at what *is* and allowing God to work in our lives with those realities. God neither makes mistakes nor does He arbitrarily deal out pain. He gives purpose to our suffering, and such a perspective can bring great comfort to those who grieve.

*A Variety of Ways to Offer Comfort.* The outline of the training program (chap. 13) gives further insights into ways to offer comfort; but let me also say that as you discover God's comfort in your own life, you will have a storehouse of comfort to offer those who are hurting.

Search your heart. Let the perspective offered in the pages of this book generate your own awareness of suffering and sweet comfort. Your ability to offer care doesn't come from being expertly trained, it comes from your own understanding of life, truth, and love.

# SECTION FOUR:
## Establishing a Ministry of Care and Concern within the Church

Therefore, as God's chosen people, holy and dearly loved, clothe yourselves with compassion, kindness, humility, gentleness and patience. Bear with each other and forgive whatever grievances you may have against one another. Forgive as the Lord forgave you. And over all these virtues put on love, which binds them all together in perfect unity.

Let the peace of Christ rule in your hearts, since as members of one body you were called to peace. And be thankful. Let the word of Christ dwell in you richly as you teach and admonish one another with all wisdom, and as you sing psalms, hymns and spiritual songs with gratitude in your hearts to God. And whatever you do, whether in word or deed, do it all in the name of the Lord Jesus, giving thanks to God the Father through Him.

Colossians 3:12-17

# ELEVEN

## A Willing Heart and
## a Desire to Serve

While it is easy to see the need for care and concern within the church, it is not always easy to determine who should be commissioned to meet that need. Members of individual churches generally desire the pastor's support, but no pastor can reach deeply or consistently into the hurt of every member. The ministry of comfort is a corporate one, each member supplying what he or she is able.

What does it take to be a caregiver? What are the qualifications? Is caregiving something that is best done by the pastor, deacons, and elders, or can a layperson offer that ministry? How can we, as a church, minister to the people in our midst who need the comfort that God has made available to His beloved?

As hard as comforting may seem to the observer, the requirements are quite simple. It truly takes a willingness to be involved and the desire to serve someone in need.

### A Willing Heart

As simple as it sounds, one of the most important qualifications for offering comfort is a willingness to be involved in the life of someone who is hurting. Don't be fooled by the simplicity, however. It isn't as easy as it sounds.

At first, many of us are anxious to be involved, but suffering rarely ends when we tire of its company. When we commit to offering comfort, we commit to a timetable with a mind all of its own. Sometimes a person's need arises in a timely fashion, but sometimes it comes when we are busy, tired, or simply "fed up."

Remember when Jesus sent the Twelve out into the world two by two? Their mission: to minister to people in the power and name of Jesus Christ (Mark 6:6-13). They went out a bit timid, but came back filled with stories of *their* accomplishments. Jesus invited them away for a while to rest and share their experiences. The rest of the story is a familiar one.

> He [Jesus] said to them, "Come with Me by your-selves to a quiet place and get some rest." So they went away by themselves in a boat to a solitary place. But many who saw them leaving recognized them and ran on foot from all the towns and got there ahead of them. When Jesus landed and saw a large crowd, He had compassion on them, because they were like sheep without a shepherd. So He began teaching them many things.
>
> By this time it was late in the day, so His disciples came to Him. "This is a remote place," they said, "and it's already very late. Send the people away so they can go to the surrounding countryside and vil-lages and buy themselves something to eat."
>
> But He answered, "You give them something to eat."
>
> They said to Him, "That would take eight months of a man's wages! Are we to go and spend that much on bread and give it to them to eat?" (Mark 6:36-37)

The disciples were willing to give of themselves when the giving was new and their power astounding. They enjoyed the comfort-giving ministry as long as it was on their terms. When they thought they were going to have an opportunity to rest, howev-er, the willingness changed. There came all those people again—people who were always looking for Jesus and His mir-acles. The disciples wanted a break, but the crowds didn't seem to care.

I don't blame the disciples at all! They had legitimately worked hard, and they wanted a break from their duties just for a little while. Jesus, however, didn't see the needed break in quite the same way.

> When Jesus landed and saw a large crowd, He had
> compassion on them, because they were like sheep
> without a shepherd (Mark 6:34).

The crowds came for physical relief, but our Lord saw something
much deeper that moved Him. He saw a wandering people who
couldn't care for themselves. He saw people who were lost and
alone, and He had the remedy for their pain.

A willingness to offer comfort carries with it a sense of responsibility and sacrifice. Caregivers are aware that comforting
takes time.

### A Desire to Serve

We live in a world where service is a rare commodity. "Service
with a smile" has been replaced, in most cases, by "I hope you
can find it yourself." In an effort to decrease the costs and
increase the profits, we have made service something we recall
only from the distant past. In recent decades, people have come
to suspect that if they don't take care of themselves, no one else
will. This is a sad turn of events.

My father owned and operated gasoline stations and car
washes while I was growing up. I loved going with him and
making the rounds, helping out where I was allowed and watch-
ing all the people who came in to be served by "Chape Chapin."
My father was and has continued to be motivated by a strong
belief that we should serve one another. He is correct.

> Your attitude should be the same as that of Jesus
> Christ: who, being in very nature God, did not con-
> sider equality with God something to be grasped, but
> made Himself nothing, taking the very nature of a
> servant, being made in human likeness. And being
> found in appearance as a man, He humbled Himself
> and became obedient to death—even death on a
> cross! (Phil. 2:5-8)

The Son of God took the very nature of a servant. He stepped into
this world, in the form of a human being, to serve us obediently in
ways we did not even know we needed. His service was a function
of His attitude. It was not a "limited time only" offer.

97

COUNSELORS, COMFORTERS, AND FRIENDS

Having an attitude of service is different than choosing to serve someone at a specific point in time. An attitude of service implies an "inside out" choice to love one another as Jesus so graciously loved us.

The disciples were in for a surprise in the days and weeks that preceded our Savior's death on the cross. At a time when His upcoming crucifixion should have preoccupied His mind, He chose, instead, to serve. I wish I could have been at that Last Supper when so much was at stake yet so few were aware.

> The evening meal was being served, and the devil had already prompted Judas Iscariot, son of Simon, to betray Jesus. Jesus knew that the Father had put all things under His power, and that He had come from God and was returning to God; so He got up from the meal, took off His outer clothing, and wrapped a towel around His waist. After that, He poured water into a basin and began to wash His disciples' feet, drying them with the towel that was wrapped around Him (John 13:2-5).

The scene was a tender one. In preparation for His own suffering and death, our Lord took personal comfort from serving the ones He loved. It was after this time of real sacrifice and service that He gave them a new command: "Love one another. As I have loved you, so you must love one another. All men will know that you are My disciples if you love one another" (John 13:34-35).

Was "love one another" truly a new command? Hadn't we heard those words before?

The "newness" came in the simple qualifying words that followed the familiar command: "As I have loved you." Jesus was about to lay down His life for His friends, and He prepared them for His death by washing their feet.

## Obstacles to Being a Caregiver

The last thing I want to do is discourage anyone from reaching out, but I do want to make the invitation to reach out a realistic one. There are certain obstacles to caregiving that need to be explored as we establish ministries of care and concern.

98

*Dependency.* When a person is hurting, the comforter often knows better what is needed for healing than the hurting person knows. Simply because suffering is often a severe shock to the personal system, the sufferer depends on caregivers for guidance and instruction. Such dependency often feels unnatural and uncomfortable to the caregiver.

Dependency can also continue to pose a problem. If the caregiver is quite involved, it is possible that the hurting person will want to "hold on." This doesn't have to be a problem, particularly if the caregiver is aware of the potential feelings of dependence. The solution is rather simple.

If you begin to feel as if the sufferer is depending too heavily on your visits, advice, or concern, simply talk about those feelings. You can use this as a way of helping that person get back into the role of responsibility.

Please don't avoid the hurting one without any explanation. Such behavior generally increases his or her pain. Model a relationship of talking through the feelings rather than pretending they don't exist.

*Helplessness.* Perhaps one of the most difficult obstacles is the helplessness we feel when we see someone hurting and we can do little to alleviate the pain. The best thing I know to say in response is that pain isn't "bad." We must retrain our thinking to include God's perspective. He uses the suffering in our lives to teach, to mold, to humble, to increase our faith, to enable us to receive His comfort and, in turn, comfort others. He knows exactly what He is doing and why.

Though we feel helpless, it is best to stick with that feeling and realize that, in essence, we are helpless to change another's circumstances or make another's decisions. Yet, while we may be helpless, God is helpful and never at a loss for what to do. He uses us to bring comfort, not to take away the suffering.

*Fear of Personal Pain.* I have long observed a certain happening in the hospital room or the home of a person newly operated on or diagnosed with a difficult disease. Family and friends crowd around, eager to help and support. Flowers and well wishes abound, and everyone seems motivated to support the loved one who is undergoing the loss, as long as the illness or recovery is short-lived.

If, however, the prognosis is grim or the rehabilitation slow and unpredictable, the support of loved ones begins to dwindle. Is this because we don't care? No. It is because we are afraid.

When you sit beside the bed of a terminally or chronically ill person, it is difficult to pretend that life isn't costly. Right before our eyes there is testimony to the final toll that life takes, and such a view is very unnerving to the unprepared.

If you are going to be a caregiver, prepare yourself with an easy exercise (not guaranteed to give you all the answers, just to make you think!). Take a pen and some paper and write a response to the following questions.

"If you were chronically or terminally ill, what do you think you would be feeling? What do you think you would be needing from your family and friends? If you were severely depressed or had just lost a loved one, what do you think you would be feeling? What do you think you would be needing from your family and friends?" I think you get the idea.

Try to put yourself in the sufferer's place. It isn't that you'll suddenly know everything about that person, but you will have done some thinking about the reality of suffering itself. It will move the pain a little closer to home, which is exactly what we fear in the first place.

*Weariness.* Just as the disciples grew weary of offering comfort, so do we. We often start big and finish small, feeling guilty for not completing the job we had originally set out to do.

What happens when the caregiver just feels tired of giving? The first part of the solution is simply this: Don't be surprised when you run out of energy. There is nothing unusual about growing weary in the midst of ministering, so you need not burden yourself with feelings of guilt.

Second, talk to the hurting person about your own limitations. As simple as such a suggestion sounds, it can save much expectation and stress on the relationship. Tell the person, "I can stay for an hour today. I'm feeling a bit tired and need to go home and rest."

The same advice applies to setting limits in order to protect your other relationships. Talk to the hurting person about your life, family, and friends. Share important events and fun times. Don't hesitate to say, "I can't come by tomorrow. I have a baseball game to attend."

This helps the sufferer regain a perspective of the bigger

world. It also helps the hurting one accept the commitments and interests of others.

Sometimes we feel guilty for having fun while another is in pain, but the hurting person will benefit from life going on just as much as the caregiver benefits from the same.

*Inadequacy.* Feelings of inadequacy are not all that different from feelings of helplessness, but I'm using inadequacy here as the struggle that often keeps us from getting involved in the first place.

"I'm not very good at visiting people who are ill." "I'm never sure what to say." "I haven't been through that, so I don't know how to help." "Someone else can probably help this person much more than I can." "I don't really have the kind of gift to help people who are suffering." "I don't know that family very well."

Do any of these statements sound familiar? When we feel inadequate, we often avoid getting involved. And that is a tragedy.

You don't have to have been through something to help someone else. You don't have to know what to say. You don't even have to be that good at talking to or caring for someone who is ill or grieving. The simple criteria? A willing heart and a desire to serve.

We are all inadequate, and suffering tends to bring our inadequacies into focus. There is no need to postpone comfort bearing until we feel in control of the situation. In fact, the best caregivers are those who know that it isn't what they say or do that matters; it's who they are.

*The Definition of Success.* Most of us don't mind working hard if the hard work produces what we call "success." Sometimes people are steered away from caregiving because there is no guarantee as to the results.

Caregiving is successful living in and of itself. Being a comforter does not hinge on acceptable results; it hinges on bringing comfort to someone in need.

Sometimes the person we are comforting dies from an illness or an accident. Sometimes the person we are comforting continues to grieve or suffer from depression. Sometimes the sufferer experiences the kind of pain that never truly goes away. Such results do not have any correlation with the value or purpose of the service.

We enter the caregiving role to reach out to someone else with the kind of comfort we ourselves have received from God. If we reach out with comfort, then that is success. The relationship is the focal point, the end results or possible changes are secondary.

### Benefits of Caregiving

The benefits of reaching out are more numerous than we can name in a short space, but there are a few benefits that are worthy of mention.

*Simple Obedience.* As sterile or parental as this might sound, there are few things more fulfilling than knowing that we are obeying God. He called us to love and care for one another, so when we are doing just that, the feelings of satisfaction are tremendous.

We generally don't mind obeying when God asks us to do something we want do do, but when He asks us to do something that is difficult or uncomfortable, our preference is to make excuses for ourselves and avoid the calling.

There are those who are given special gifts of mercy, but all of us are called to be merciful. It is not the job of only the pastor, elders, or deacons to provide comfort; it is the privilege of every believer.

*Worth.* When we reach out to comfort someone who is hurting, we reach into the very life of a person who is doubting personal worth and significance. As you are well aware, when people, health, jobs, or other things we value are taken away for whatever reason, we hurt. We feel a sense of worthlessness.

When a person steps in, ready to love us in spite of the brokenness and unanswered questions, we begin to see our worth once more. We begin to remember our significance.

God blessed Elijah with a sense of worth. Jesus returned Peter to a sense of worth. And our Lord gave sinner after sinner a deep awareness of worth before God. In fact, it is because of our worth in God's eyes that He sent His Son to die for us.

*Friendship.* Which one of us doesn't desire friendship? Especially valuable are the friendships that last—the ones that are based on mutual respect and love. Such is a by-product of caregiving.

When you first walk into the home or hospital room of someone who is hurting, the relationship may feel awkward. The hurting ones know you are there as a representative of the church. They might even be disappointed that the pastor couldn't come.

Hold on! Once you begin to get involved and open up, the friendship will flower. And the kind of friendship strengthened through pain or loss is a friendship with lifetime potential. Remember, you're sharing in one of that family's most strategic moments. And they will not quickly forget your smile, your touch, your willingness, your honesty, your availability.

*Personal Growth.* Even though we don't go into caregiving with personal growth in mind, it happens. It comes quickly and consistently throughout the course of our relationships.

At the simplest level, we grow because we are stretched beyond our earlier limits. Since we are faced with trying to bring comfort to someone who is devastated, we must draw on that deep well that is available to us through the Holy Spirit.

On a given day, we operate within the limits of our own experience. In caregiving, we operate not only within our limits but outside of those limits, exercising faith, love, patience, and hope.

We learn to see through God's eyes instead of our own; thus, the growth. We draw on a resource deeper than we've known.

A by-product of our own loving service is a deeper walk with God. He is there, and He is our source of comfort.

### "Let Me Count the Ways"

There are so many ways that caregiving benefits the church. In fact, once you taste the experience of offering comfort, you'll continue to reach out. In a sense, I see caregiving as one of the main ways the church can set herself apart.

We have solutions; perhaps not the kind that a hurting person might want at the moment, but the kind that will last and last and last. As believers, we have perspective and we have purposes for the sufferings we endure.

Get ready to serve. Be part of the caregiving group in your church. Be prepared to grow and gain more than you've ever imagined.

# TWELVE

## Recruiting
## the
## Volunteers

**Making the Need Known**

The first step in training volunteers is getting the message out in church. People are only intellectually aware of the need for caregivers. In fact, most church members think the pastor and other members of the church staff have visitation under control.

The selection process begins with the church staff. If pastors make the need known to church members, then the body has a chance to respond to that need and begin to work in this area. The following are some ideas for exposing the congregation to the need.

*Hearing Personal Stories.* There is nothing more convincing than the personal testimony of family members or individuals who have been recipients of caregiving at a critical point in life. During a special worship service or, perhaps, in several consecutive ones, schedule personal testimonies. Invite those who have struggled through depression, grief, or the strain of an illness to express the experience and the value of support within the body.

*Exploring God's Message of Comfort.* There are a variety of ways to show the congregation the power of comfort. Perhaps the testimony of those in pain is the clearest way. Yet another important method is teaching members of the church about the comfort God gives. The pastor can open up God's Word and explore the variety of ways God has brought comfort to His people through the years.

Perhaps a series of sermons on comforting will introduce the church to this ministry. Perhaps an informal time of sharing when believers are encouraged to talk about God's comfort in their lives will open the congregation to the idea.

Whatever creative method is chosen, spending time in God's Word can only make clearer His comforting ways and our need to extend that comfort to others.

*Educating the Church on the Needs.* It is important to educate the congregation on the various needs of the people. We are accustomed to certain needs we all share in common, but there are a number of problems a church might confront that are uncomfortable and unknown to the majority.

When we don't relate to a certain struggle, we tend to pretend it doesn't exist. When that happens, those members of the community who struggle from that particular pain remain silent and uncomforted.

It is important that the pastoral staff work on educating the body of believers concerning the variety of struggles that are part of our world today. We are better at dealing with illness and death than we are at dealing with depression, alcoholism, teenage pregnancy, the requirements of single parenting, divorce, abuse, or AIDS. The congregation needs help expanding the horizons of awareness.

In short, there are struggles that certain members of the congregation face, and it is helpful to educate the wider audience in how to offer comfort to those who face a particular pain.

*The Need of the Pastoral Staff for Help.* As God's comfort is explored, it is important that the pastoral staff express their need for help in offering comfort to God's hurting people. Again, sometimes members of the church hesitate to step in when they feel it is the pastor's job.

Two things are required to educate the church concerning the pastor's need for help. One is easy, one is not.

First, and most difficult, is the need for the pastor to "let go" and allow others to bear part of a load that the pastor is both trained and geared to bear. This is difficult because nowhere in the workplace is control any more a problem than in the ministry.

Forgive my boldness for a moment, but take it from one who is involved in full-time ministry—we are trained to be responsible and to bear the responsibility of ministering to God's people. There is nothing wrong with bearing that load, but it is critical that we learn to use the gifts of other people in our churches. We don't have to do it all for the work to be done well.

Each week, the pastoral staff receives calls for prayer requests, surgeries, tragedies, marriages, and deaths. Each week the pastoral staff makes a concerted effort to reach out to those people with God's comfort.

While there is nothing quite like the visit of someone we love and trust, it is impossible for the pastoral staff to follow up on all of the needs, providing ongoing comfort and care. If the leaders of the church can work out the responsibility issue, then the door is open for inviting caregivers from the larger community of believers.

The second step is really quite simple. Once the pastor or staff has agreed to welcome help, then making that need known starts the wheels rolling.

## The Job Itself

Before people volunteer to offer comfort, they will want to know exactly what such a job entails. Simply put, an individual, couple, or family will be assigned another individual, couple, or family who is experiencing a particular need at that point in time. The caregiver is then asked to make contact with the assigned person, couple, or family and continue contact as long as the caregiving is needed.

For instance, a caregiver might be assigned to a single-parent home where the mother has been ill for some time and is now suffering from depression. That caregiver will call the mother, and if she is interested in having a friend in the church, will set up a time to see her. At that meeting, the caregiver will determine the needs of the situation and support that woman through her time of difficulty.

This is not necessarily a relationship where the physical needs of the person are met, though such a ministry might be offered as part of the caregiving. Instead, this is a ministry of talking, praying, encouraging, and suggesting. This is a friendship with resources of comfort.

Depending on the size and setup of the church, the assigned caregiver will present a periodic update to the pastor or the pastoral staff so all can stay abreast of the situation and better understand the needs of the congregation. This way the caregiver can also ask for suggestions or ideas for bringing comfort in that particular situation.

Should the pastoral staff still visit and stay in touch with the sufferer? Absolutely. The lay ministry of comfort doesn't take the place of the pastor's concern; it increases the pastor's ability to show that concern.

### Identifying the Caregivers

There are several ways to discover those who are willing to be part of a ministry of comfort, and that discovery depends largely on the size of the congregation.

If the church body is rather small, then the pastor may already know people in the church who would be willing to reach out and help others. Those who have been through a previous pain are often the most willing and sensitive caregivers, and that is certainly a place to begin.

If the church body is large, then the discovery of caregivers takes a little more leg work. The following are suggested ways for conducting the search:

*Sunday School Classes and Existing Support Groups.* Most leaders or sponsors of a particular Sunday School class know the members of that class and can identify people who are, by nature, comforters. The pastor can ask the Sunday School leaders either to provide a list of possibilities or conduct a minisearch within the class, asking for volunteers.

If the church is particularly large and decentralized around the support groups or Sunday School classes, then the caregiving itself may best be established as a closed ministry within that group. If this is the decision of the staff, then provisions need to be made to offer comfort to people who are not members of a specialized group within the church.

*Conducting a Survey.* While this sounds a bit dry on the surface, it can actually be a big help to the pastoral staff. The staff can put together an information package and ask members to answer the questions, giving thought and prayer to the various needs within the church. After the survey has been completed, the staff can discover those with special needs, gifts, and services.

107

The survey should ideally follow a series of messages or testimonials about comfort-giving within the church. When the congregation is more aware of the types of pain people feel and the need for comfort, they will likely be more responsive to being comforters.

While the following list is not exhaustive, it gives a general format that can be followed. Consideration should be given to particular needs of congregations based on location, cultural mix, age of members, and so forth.

For instance, a congregation with many young couples might need to list miscarriages or birth defects as one of the possible experiences of pain.

A congregation with older adults might want to check insurance problems or fear of living alone as one of the possible experiences.

The survey is informational in nature, identifying key people who have experienced difficulties and who want to help others as a result of their experiences. The following is an example of such a member survey:

### Member Survey: Sharing the Gift of Comfort

We believe a vital part of our church ministry lies in its individual members and their willingness to offer comfort to those in pain. Please complete the following survey, and be sure to indicate if you are currently in need of encouragement in any particular area.

Name: _____
Address: _____
Phone: _____ # of family members: _____
Current involvements within the church: _____
_____
_____

Please indicate with a check in the appropriate column whether you or your family have experienced any of the following, would be open to comforting someone who's experiencing any of the following, or currently need help for any of the following:

| Painful Experience | Personal/ Indirect Experience | Willing to Help | Need Help |
|---|---|---|---|
| divorce | | | |
| a change in job | ___ | ___ | ___ |
| a physical move | ___ | ___ | ___ |
| personal illness— chronic or other | ___ | ___ | ___ |
| aging | ___ | ___ | ___ |
| aging parents | ___ | ___ | ___ |
| death—spouse | ___ | ___ | ___ |
| death—loved one | ___ | ___ | ___ |
| death—child | ___ | ___ | ___ |
| serious illness—spouse | ___ | ___ | ___ |
| serious illness— loved one | ___ | ___ | ___ |
| serious illness—child | ___ | ___ | ___ |
| discipline problems—child | ___ | ___ | ___ |
| learning disabilities | ___ | ___ | ___ |
| automobile accident | ___ | ___ | ___ |
| financial difficulties | ___ | ___ | ___ |
| pregnancy out of wedlock | ___ | ___ | ___ |
| marital problems | ___ | ___ | ___ |
| single parenting | ___ | ___ | ___ |
| surgery—self or family | ___ | ___ | ___ |

Though the survey itself won't tell the pastoral staff all that they need to know, it will begin the process of identifying what help is available in the body so the needs of hurting individuals can be matched with the experiences of those who have received comfort in their moments of pain.

Again, you don't need to have experienced divorce to help someone who has just suffered through a divorce; you simply must be willing to get involved and care. At the same time, some of the best comforters are those who have experienced similar pains.

### Training the Caregivers
There are a variety of ways to train people within the church to offer comfort and support to those in need. I have included an outline of my training program as a model (chap. 13), but feel

109

COUNSELORS, COMFORTERS, AND FRIENDS

free to modify the program to personally fit the design of your church.

The training I advise follows the ideas presented in this book.

*The All-Important Element: Attitude.* Regardless of the elements you might want to include in your training, keep one very important thought in mind: The kind of care we give is a direct reflection of what we believe. Let me explain.

My whole purpose in writing the first three sections of this book is to deal with this very issue: our attitude toward painful experiences.

If we believe that suffering is a mistake or that God never wants us to suffer, then our own beliefs will limit the kind of comfort we offer. Instead of praying for strength for the person, we'll be praying for pain's removal. Instead of praying for wisdom, we'll be praying for everything to return to "normal."

The most critical aspect of the training program is our attitude. If you unlock the fears of the volunteers and help them see God's comfort in the midst of the pain, then the kind of care they offer will be tremendously comforting. Spend a lot of time on attitude, and the skills will fall gracefully into place.

*A Few Important Points.* As you tailor-make the training program for your church, there are a few elements that need to be remembered and stressed. Here is a review of those elements:

- Pain and suffering are part of living in this world. While unpleasant, they are not "enemies." God is present as we walk through our "valleys of the shadow of death." Suffering is a reality that He uses to teach, encourage, and strengthen us—and, through us, others who are in pain.

- We don't have to experience the specifics of another person's pain in order to help that person through a difficult time. We simply have to want to be there and serve others in their need. Though someone who has been through the specific problem might be best suited, that is not necessarily the case.

- Even if members of the congregation are, at first, a little hesitant or resistant to anyone other than members of the pastoral staff, the hurting person or family will quickly

110

warm up to someone who truly cares. Just walk right in and begin to love. Their acceptance generally will not take long.

- Even the most dedicated pastor cannot meet all of the needs of hurting people all of the time. The volunteer caregivers aren't there to displace the pastor or pastoral staff, but to support. The pastoral staff can rest easy knowing that those who are hurting are receiving steady care.

- The caregivers don't need to put hours into their comforting, though most will. The key to offering comfort isn't in "time," it is in the quality of care. Ten honest minutes is better than an hour of nervous chatter or avoidance of the pain.

- Often, the family and friends of the sufferer need the encouragement every bit as much as the person who is struggling. The caregiver will be a friend and support to the family as well as to the sufferer.

- Hope cannot be lost or tampered with in any way. We can feel hopeless in the face of certain circumstances, but hope is firmly rooted in Jesus' ministry of redemption. Don't hesitate to speak candidly with a sufferer and to teach the family and friends to speak candidly with one another. The sufferer cannot "lose hope."

# THIRTEEN

## A Sample Training Program

The training program can be done in any way that fits the schedule of the caregivers and church staff. It is usually best to conduct the training program in at least four sessions, giving people the opportunity to think and ask questions.

An all-day session on Saturday, sessions two nights in a row, morning or evening sessions over several weeks, a special Sunday School or Wednesday evening class—all of these are possibilities, depending on the dynamics of the church.

It is my suggestion that you offer a training session at least every six months. Thus, as the word of the program spreads and the needs of the congregation change, you will have a continual stream of people entering the caregiving program.

Finally, the training program is general enough to offer help all the way from physical problems to alcohol abuse. The basics lie in attitude and perspective. This program can support virtually all needs and pains experienced in your church. Everyone needs a friend.

### Giving the Program a Name
Though this is not a necessary move, often a name helps a program stay in people's minds. The name gives the congregation something to remember and identify with.

One name that is popular in training programs I've conducted is "REACH." This acronym stands for "Reaching Out With Encouragement, Advice, Compassion, and Hope." Though

112

those elements are not the only ones involved in offering comfort, they do describe the basic needs of those who hurt.

If and when you choose a name, keep in mind the impression
that the name will make upon the church body. You might even
ask the congregation for suggestions.

### Including the Church Leaders

An important part of the program is including those leaders
within the church who have been caregiving or praying for
years. Elders, deacons, deaconesses, Sunday School teachers,
and other church leaders will benefit from the training and from
getting to know the various laypeople in the church who are
offering their services to those in need.

It is not that all of the church leaders will take part in the
actual program. It is, instead, that taking part in the training will
help those leaders to be aware of what is happening in the
church. Their involvement will also encourage the involvement
of others.

### Using the Book as a Guide

Certainly, if the words contained in this book could help not
only the pastoral staff but also the members of the congregation,
that would please me greatly. As a sufferer myself, I have a great
interest in the church utilizing her gifts and her great resource of
love in order to reach out to those in need.

This book could become the starting point for training
caregivers. Allow them several weeks to read the perspectives
and think through what is presented, and then use their questions and insights to launch the training itself.

### Outside Support-Group Ministries

It is my guess that most churches are understaffed and saddled
with a long list of ministries that need doing. I see the ministry
of caregiving itself as a critical foundation for the church, but I
well know that most churches aren't equipped to have share
groups meet the variety of needs expressed among their
members.

Support groups in the community can provide much support
to the ministry of comfort and concern within the church. For
instance, if someone is in need of the professional services of an

organization like Hospice, that should be encouraged and the contacts made available.

At the same time, the family seeking Hospice support needs the continuing ministry of caregiving from the church. The lay volunteer will simply continue the friendship and help wherever possible.

As the ministry grows in the church, the members themselves will begin to meet the needs of others who are hurting in a particular area. At that point, they might desire to start a support group to supplement their healing.

Take this ministry one step at a time. And don't fear getting bogged down in a number of groups. As they form, you can assign caregivers to the groups who are already involved in the lives of the members represented. (Chap. 16 deals further with the support-group ministry.)

# The Program Itself

## Session 1
## Caregiving in the Church

**Introduction:**

We are here to understand better how to support people in their time of need. The thought seems overwhelming at times, especially in the face of an accident, terminal illness, or the death of a loved one. Yet the method is actually very simple. Reaching out to people with love is one of the basic gifts of the believer. It is the best gift you can give away! A program such as this one is a program of reaching out in love and offering advice, understanding, encouragement, comfort, hope, and truth. As we begin, it is important to explore some of the basic, though often undiscussed, ingredients of our lives: suffering, death, and grief.

Suffering, death, and grief are not words that we like to discuss or consider. They are words that represent vulnerability, lack of control, fear, and insecurity. They are experiences we avoid. Yet they are also experiences that are central to our theology, significant to our relationships with God, and essential parts of our experiences in this world.

How we see suffering, death, and grief directly affects how we respond to God in our times of need as well as how we comfort one another. It is important that we learn to see these experiences through the eyes of God.

1. The Reality of Pain in This World

   Pain is mental; it is physical; it is emotional; it is spiritual; and, at times, it is all of these elements at once. Most importantly, pain is part of living in this world. If we dismiss that very simple reality, we spend our lives avoiding not only the inevitable, but also that which God has allowed for very important reasons in the lives of His children.

   a. Pain as a result of sin: Genesis 3:8-19; Numbers 20; 2 Samuel 11–15; Matthew 27:1-10

   b. The continued promise of pain: John 14–16; 1 Peter

   c. The benefits of suffering: God's perspective

      1. Romans 5:1-5
      2. Philippians 1:27-30; 3:10
      3. Lamentations
      4. James 1:2-4
      5. 1 Peter 1:3-9
      6. Job 42:1-5
      7. 1 Peter 4:1
      8. Genesis 37–50

115

Though pain and suffering are unpleasant, they are part of the process of living in a fallen world. Sometimes our own sin causes our pain. Sometimes illness causes our pain. Sometimes the natural decay of a fallen world causes our pain. Sometimes another person's sin causes our pain. And, hard as it is to accept, sometimes God allows pain for a very specific purpose that we cannot fully comprehend.

Joseph learned tremendous lessons of faith and the sovereignty of God in his pain. Jeremiah discovered the compassions of God in his suffering and disappointment. Daniel experienced a steadfast supply of God's love. Moses knew how it felt to hurt from the effects of sin. Job had no idea what was happening to him or why, yet he learned to have eyes that see God. And our Lord, perfect as He was, still learned obedience through His suffering.

Difficulty is part of our process; it is not something to be dreaded or cast off as quickly as possible so that we can return to "normal." If, in the aftermath of suffering, we return to our former state, we have sadly missed a major point of suffering itself.

2. The Reality of Death

There are really three types of death that surface in Scripture, all of which are important to the believer. The first is the kind of spiritual death experienced first by Adam and Eve after their sin in the Garden. The second is the physical death we all endure as inhabitants of this sinful world. The third, and perhaps the most difficult for us, is the death to ourselves. We are asked, by our Lord, to die to our own ways and live in Him.

a. Spiritual death: the reality of sin: Genesis 3; Romans 3:23; 6:23.

b. Physical death

1. The reality of sin: Genesis 3; testimonies of Scripture

2. "O Death, where is your victory?" 1 Corinthians 15; Colossians 3:1-10; Romans 5:17-19

c. Dying to self: the command of our Lord

1. The example of Jesus: John 12:23-28; Philippians 2:5-11; Luke 22:42

2. The responsibility/privilege of the believer: Philippians 3:4-10, 17-21; Mark 10:17-31; Colossians 3:1-10; John 12:23-28.

In short, our attitude toward death makes such a difference. Even though we know that physical death has no power over the believer, we still act as if we fear its power and as if death will lead us into disappointment. Physical death, for the believer, is going home! It is entering into life that is truly life! (1 Tim. 6) It is finally becoming whole! It is real healing!

116

The process of dying to self is what we are asked to pursue in this world—not because God is against our fulfillment and happiness, but because He knows what will bring true fulfillment and happiness. The rich young man walked away physically full, but internally and eternally empty (Mark 10). Understanding death from God's perspective makes all the difference in our attitude in this world. Hebrews 11 says it best!

3. The Realities of Grief and Depression

When we deal with various sufferings and pains, it is not unusual at all to suffer from grief and/or depression. It may be frightening to experience these emotions or moods, but they are a normal way of responding to the pains of this world.

We tend to think of grief and depression as "negative" emotions or "unspiritual" reactions, but we could not be further from the truth when we place those emotions in such a box. Grief and depression are part of suffering, and a very important part.

a. The colorful world of emotions

Emotions aren't "positive" or "negative" in and of themselves. They are simply a part of what it means to be created in the image of God. Some emotions feel better than others, and we can do very negative things as a result of our feelings, but the emotions themselves are ways of expressing our responses to life's circumstances.

1. List as many emotions as you can. Think of times you have felt those various emotions.

2. Discuss the various "myths" associated with emotions, as well as why you think we find it so difficult to express ourselves through our feelings.

b. The reality of grief

Grief is an emotional response, generally associated with a particular event or loss. It is a painful emotion that is very real. Discuss when you grieve and how you express your grief.

1. God's grief: Genesis 6:5-8
2. The grief of our Lord: John 12:27-28; Luke 22:39-44; Isaiah 53
3. The grief of Mary, Martha, and Jesus: John 11
4. Peter's grief: John 19:21
5. Grief of the disciples: John 16
6. David's grief: Psalm 51; 2 Samuel 1

c. The reality of depression

Depression is a bit longer, wider, and deeper, than grief, though it is defined in much the same way. Generally we become depressed when there are several factors in our lives causing us grief. Such factors might include the loss of a loved one, the loss of a dream, financial difficulties, or painful memories.

Clinical depression is often treated with both medication and counseling, but the kind of depression many experience is best treated with love, concern, listening, and much patience.

God's pattern with His beloved is not to treat us harshly when we suffer from depression, but to treat us, instead, with kindness and compassion.

1. Elijah's depression: 1 Kings 18–19
2. Job's depression: the Book of Job, particularly Job 3, 6, 10, 19, and 42
3. Jeremiah's depression: Lamentations

d. Signs and symptoms of grief and depression
Although not inclusive of all signs and symptoms, the following list will help identify the pain:

1. Crying
2. Loss of/or increased appetite
3. Feeling of shock or disbelief
4. Nervous or obsessive behaviors
5. Sexual disinterest/dysfunction
6. Inability to make decisions
7. Anger (turned inward or outward)
8. Difficulty maintaining relationships
9. Lethargy
10. Short attention span
11. Lack of interest in spiritual things
12. Increased interest in spiritual things
13. Need to talk about the loss
14. Lack of interest in activities
15. Lack of concern for personal care
16. Sleepless nights

Add, for depression, more than one of the above symptoms as well as the possibility of the following:

17. Hopelessness
18. Loss of perspective
19. Irrational fears
20. Sleeplessness or excessive periods of sleep
21. Thoughts of suicide or death
22. Harmful personal behaviors (scratching self, pulling out hair, etc.)
23. Loss of perspective, past and future
24. A desire to "give up"

25. A feeling of abandonment by God or total insignificance in His eyes

e. Ways to comfort during grief and depression

Again this list is not exhaustive, but it does give some suggestions for ministering to those who are suffering from grief or depression.

1. Don't "pity" the person
2. Help the person to regain perspective
3. Be patient
4. Just "be there"
5. Listen
6. Accept the person and the pain
7. Don't try to "fix"; help the person to begin to accept responsibility
8. Help the person identify the loss
9. Help the person begin to accept the loss
10. Encourage expression of emotions
11. Encourage open communication among family members and friends
12. Encourage the writing of thoughts and feelings or the recording them on tape
13. Encourage exercise and a healthy diet, and help the family understand their importance
14. Encourage the person to resume a "normal" schedule
15. Speak truth (God's comfort and Word)
16. Be honest in your relationship and conversation
17. Pray for and with, encouraging the person to be up to date with God
18. Offer the truth about forgiveness
19. Encourage honesty with the children

For depression, several of the following suggestions might also help:

20. Help the person identify the sources of the depression
21. Check regularly for signs of suicidal thoughts or actions
22. Encourage a visit to a medical doctor
23. Talk about yesterday's joys and help the person begin to dream again about tomorrow
24. Discourage long periods of being alone
25. DO NOT attempt to give easy answers
26. Help the person set small, "bite size" goals

# Session 2
## The Comforts of Jesus

### Introduction

When we think about comforting people in need, we think about "doing" something. For instance, we might go and visit someone, prepare food, offer to care for the children, or provide transportation. We think about comforting those who suffer through "doing" things on their behalf.

Think about God's comfort for a moment. Paul told the Corinthian church that we comfort others the way God has comforted us. How does God offer comfort to His people? How does God comfort you?

1. The Lord of Comfort
   a. Mark 5:1-20: The demon-possessed man is given responsibility in the community
   b. Mark 5:24-34: The woman who's been bleeding is touched and accepted
   c. Mark 5:21-43: Jairus is given an opportunity to "just believe"
   d. John 4:1-42: The woman at the well is searched, fully known, and fully accepted
   e. Luke 7:36-50: The prostitute is forgiven and rewarded for her love
   f. John 11:1-44: Jesus speaks with Martha, cries with Mary, and gives Lazarus a chance to mature
   g. John 14–16: The disciples are comforted with truth
   h. John 17: The disciples are comforted with prayer
   i. 1 Kings 19: Elijah is fed by angels, comforted in a whisper, and given help for his fears
   j. Lamentations 3: Jeremiah is given new compassion every morning
   k. John 9: The blind man is given significance for the first time

God doesn't comfort us simply by "doing." He comforts us by "being" all that He was and is and ever will be. He comforts us by His character and love, by time spent listening, supporting, providing, touching, and caring. He is not always busy "doing," but He is always busy "being."

2. Lessons of Comfort

   Think, now, of all the ways God comforts His people. Wherever possible, associate a life example from Scripture to open your eyes to the ministry of comfort.

# Session 3
## The Art of Bearing Comfort

## Introduction

Just as we have seen God's comfort, we can comfort others from the storehouse of what we've experienced with Him. Be creative in your comforting. Be kind, be aware, and learn to be sensitive to the situation. It is not what you do that makes the difference; it is who you are.

If you've never allowed God to comfort you, or if you never stopped to notice His methods, it may be difficult for you to offer His comfort to others. He is the source of comfort, the One who knows who we are and what we need.

1. Offering Comfort to Those in Need: 2 Corinthians 1
   a. Give the gift of *you*: Psalm 139
      We often forget just how important we are to the ministry of comfort. We tend to feel untrained and, therefore, inadequate to reach out. Since God has searched and known us, He has given us the ministry of loving one another. *You* are the best part of the gift of comfort.
   b. Be there; be with: Philippians 2:19-29; 1–2 Timothy
      One of the greatest comforts you can give begins with just being there. You don't have to have any great advice. You don't need any quick solutions. Being with the person says you care and you are willing to bear part of the pain. Such love is the greatest ingredient of comfort.
   c. Don't try to "fix": 2 Corinthians 12; 1–2 Timothy; Job 2:11-13; John 14–17
      "Fixing" is an inbred tendency in us. Since we feel helpless when someone hurts, we set out to fix the problem. Offering God's comfort isn't offering a solution. It is offering, instead, encouragement, faith, and perspective, so that God is free to move, teach, and love.

      When we are bent on trying to remove the pain, we miss the purpose of the pain and the depth of God's comfort. Fixing assumes there is some mistake. God has purpose in our pains. They are not mistakes in His eyes.
   d. Give the gift of time: quality vs. quantity
      We tend to think that caregiving takes a chunk of time. Evaluating our own commitments, we shy away from anything that will cause conflict and even greater stress.

      Offering comfort takes time, but not measured in quantity. The time comforting takes is of quality. When you're with the person, make eye contact, touch, let silence have its place, walk beside. Five or ten minutes of peaceful relationship is worth hours of busyness or idle conversation.

If you can't stay long, let that be known, right away. "Hi! I'm sorry to say I can't stay long today, but I want the time we share to be for you. While I'm here, nothing is more important than you." If you're running behind schedule, simply call and say, "I'm so sorry I'm running behind schedule. I think I'll wait until tomorrow to come by because I want my time with you to be unstressed, not hurried."

Honesty goes a long way. The gift of time is simply this: When you are with the person, then you are *with* the person — not thinking about dinner or the next meeting or some responsibility you've forgotten. It is the quality of time that counts.

e. Touch: Mark 5:24-30

One of the greatest gifts of comfort is simple touch. Rubbing a person's feet or head while that person is in physical pain, offering a hug or a hand when someone is suffering from grief or depression, walking in the hospital room and reaching out to the one who is ill and to the family. Touch expresses concern. It shows that you have eyes to see beyond the suffering to the person inside.

f. Listen and share: John 11; 14–17

Jesus did a lot of listening; we tend to do a lot of talking! Particularly when we feel insecure about a situation, silence makes us feel awkward and compels us to fill up the space.

Practice listening. Enjoy the silence. Share from your own experiences. Allow unspoken words and actions to work their wonder.

g. Accept the person in pain: John 4; Mark 5

We don't have to condone or approve of the pain in order to accept the person who is suffering. Jesus often disapproved of actions, but He offered comfort in His acceptance of the person.

h. Encourage emotional expression

Emotions themselves aren't "positive" or "negative," "good" or "bad"; they simply "are." Encourage the person in pain to express the emotions inside.

i. Offer and encourage forgiveness: Luke 7:36-50; John 21:15-19; 2 Corinthians 2:5-11; 5:11-21

Even though we may have nothing to do with the person's pain or need, sometimes the gift of comfort reminds a person of the forgiveness available in Jesus Christ. Even if that person is knowledgeable about the theological perspective on forgiveness, it helps to have the assurance of someone "in the flesh."

Likewise, the family may need to do some forgiving. Often suffering brings up old, undealt with emotions and hurts, and the caregiver does best to encourage the family members to open up the lines of communication and clear out the old issues.

j. Encourage personal responsibility: John 5:1-15; 9; 21; Mark 5:1-20

Sometimes we feel sorry for the person in pain. Thus, we attempt to guard that person from responsibility. At times such protection is necessary—for a time; but most hurting people need a gentle shove back into the world of responsibility.

We feel sorry for ourselves when we're hurting. Life seems pointless; energy seems lost; and the mundane requirements of life seem so unimportant. Still, part of the healing process is hidden in the taking up of our responsibilities once again. It is valuable to reenter the world.

k. Offer a reminder of personal significance: Job 6; 9; Luke 10:38; John 11:1–12:1

The painful experiences of life often threaten to steal our sense of significance. Help the hurting recall their importance to their families, to the church, and to their friends.

l. Be honest: Ephesians 4:15-16, 29-32

Honesty doesn't necessarily mean telling everything you know, but it does mean presenting yourself as a person who can be trusted, believed, and confided in. Honesty is almost an atmosphere around us rather than words we might say.

We often attempt to hide news, a prognosis, or professional opinions from those who are suffering, sensing that the honesty might be too much for them to bear. The real truth is, such openness is generally too much for us to bear! We tend to cover up our own feelings of discomfort or sadness in an attempt to protect the hurting ones.

It is generally best to be who you are and to share with the sufferer most of the conversations in your own mind. Simple statements such as, "I am having a difficult time knowing how to help. I feel so helpless, and that is an uncomfortable feeling for me"; or "I hate to see you in pain"; or "I've been standing outside your door for a long time because I was afraid to see you today" are usually the best expressions of honesty you can offer.

It is important that sufferers be kept abreast of the events in their lives. It is important that sufferers be given the opportunity to make decisions about their lives and learn how to communicate with friends and family members. The gift of honesty is a rare but valuable part of comforting.

m. Offer and affirm truth: John 14–17

Truth was one of the gifts the disciples could count on Jesus giving. He spoke the truth in love to them, whether the news was happy or difficult to hear.

It seems that we often have trouble distinguishing truth from our own opinion. It helps to remember that truth is God's Word, written in the Scriptures and upon our hearts. What generally passes for truth in this world is our personal perception of reality or of a specific situation. Thus, without meaning to, we make value judgments and often conceal truth.

What is truth when someone is dying and the family doesn't want to talk about it? Perhaps it is opening up God's Word to them and reading from the Psalms or from Job or Lamentations or John. Perhaps it is describing God's perspective and painting a picture of true hope. Perhaps truth, at that moment, sounds something like this:

"I know that you are suffering as you watch your loved one in pain. And I know that you are afraid to talk about death, especially with the sufferer. I wish I could make your burden lighter, but this much I know: God is with us right now, and if physical death is in store, so is the strength to deal with that loss. If physical death is in store for your loved one, then that person is about to experience more life and more joy than you and I have ever known. Let me encourage you to think and pray about something: If you can open up and talk about your grief as a family, then everyone has the opportunity to share in one another's pain. It will be a great relief to you and to the sufferer to be able to talk about the loss and the fears. I would like to help, so I'll ask you about this again tomorrow. If you would like, I'll show you some comforting passages from Scripture that just might help you express your feelings."

By making such a statement, you have been sensitive to what the family fears, but you have also opened the door to their being able to bear one another's burdens.

Truth and the words of Scripture can take a difficult time and make it not just "bearable," but filled with faith, hope, and love.

124

n. Encourage openness among family and friends

Just a reminder to say that loved ones often have a difficult time expressing their concerns, love, and fears to one another when suffering becomes part of their lives. Even though you may not know them well, encourage a spirit of openness in the relationships, reminding them that a burden shared is much lighter than one borne alone.

Sometimes the excuse for lack of communication is, "He can't talk about the pain" or, "She isn't accepting the situation." Rarely is that the case. Generally speaking, the sufferer wants to talk about the situation, but fears burdening family and friends. As you can see, if left unattended, the conversations that need to occur are avoided because everyone is trying to protect everyone else.

Help the family members and friends learn to talk, cry, and express their anger or fears. A shared burden is truly lighter, and the grief is better resolved when kept up to date.

Family #1: "I'm so afraid he's going to stay depressed! What do I say?"

Caregiver: "Tell him what you just told me. Share your fears with him. He's part of your life, and your fears affect him just as his depression affects you."

Family #2: "The doctor says she isn't going to live very long. What do we tell her?"

Caregiver: "You tell her what the doctor said."

Family #2: "Won't she lose hope?"

Caregiver: "She may feel hopeless at first, but she can't lose hope. In fact, she's about to understand hope better than you or I understand it. Talk to her; let her cry; cry with her. If she's depressed, that is normal. We can help her through the difficult times."

Family #3: "I can't take care of my mother any more. I love her, but I have three children of my own, and I'm exhausted with trying to juggle her needs and the needs of my family. What do I say? She's going to be so upset."

Caregiver: "This is difficult, and she may indeed be upset; but you're going to have to share your struggles with your mother. I'll help you think through your options, but let her be part of that process as well. The most difficult thing for your mother will be feeling that she no longer has control over her life. Let's help her retain some responsibility and, at the same time, provide you with a solution to your juggling act."

125

Family #3: "But I feel so guilty. She took care of me for years."

Caregiver: "I understand. But you're not going to stop loving her; you're simply going to find a way to love her and your family better than you're doing right now. Your mother will grieve, but she'll grow with you as you remain open."

o. Encourage openness with health care professionals, employers, and others involved in the life of the sufferer

So many times the sufferers are afraid to ask questions of health care or other professionals. There is a built-in belief that the professionals know more than the layperson, and that the job of the layperson is to obey the advice or directives.

Most people want to know more about their situation. Greater understanding reduces fear, and sufferers should be encouraged to ask questions and seek understanding of the situation.

At the simplest level, encourage the person in pain to make a list of questions or frustrations. The same can be done for family members and friends. Help them learn to open up those lines of communication.

p. Discuss spiritual things openly (No answers are necessary!)

Most people who are suffering turn to deeper, more spiritual thoughts and questions. Talk freely about these thoughts and questions, offering ideas where you feel it is valuable or appropriate.

q. Pray "for" and pray "with": John 17; Psalms

Prayer is always a great comforter. There is a connection in prayer, both with God and the ones who are praying. Such a connection brings deep comfort.

We tend to pray for the sufferer, and that is often exactly what that person needs. We should remember, however, that praying "with" the one who is in pain gives that person the opportunity to share thoughts, emotions, needs, and fears with God. Sometimes it has been weeks or months since the sufferer has felt comfortable talking to the Father. Help them to learn to pray again; or, perhaps, for the first time. Encourage open expressions of honesty with God.

r. Be patient. Comforting takes time

2. Important things to remember
   a. There is a "bigger picture" going on than we can see
      Pain, suffering, death, and grief are not always what they seem to be at the moment. God knows what He is doing, and He never allows pain without purpose.

126

b. Help bear the burden, but do not try to lift the entire load
Galatians 5:1-6 provides this perspective. God gives us responsibility to carry, and friends to help in the process. He does not ask you or me to bear the complete load for someone else. In truth, we cannot lift their burden. What we can do is slip a hand underneath their pack and help make the load a little more bearable.

c. You are not there to "fix"; rather you are there to share in the experience, walk alongside to lend support, and don't forget to learn, both with and from

d. Emotions and emotional expressions are both normal and healthy
Encourage expression of the emotions, and seek to understand what the sufferer is feeling.

e. There is neither a right way to grieve nor a right timetable for recovery

f. This world is not our home
As attractive or comfortable as it might seem, we are aliens and strangers here, purposed yet not rooted. Our eternal joy is being home with the Lord. If we can remember this perspective, the suffering takes on a different light. (Heb. 11 and 1 Peter say this best!)

g. The mark of the believer is not how independent and self-reliant we can be; it is how we love one another
We are part of the corporate body of Christ, and we need one another. It is our suffering that makes us vulnerable and able to better understand the working together of the eternal body of believers ( 1 Cor. 12–13; 2 Cor. 12).

h. The success we have in comforting or encouraging someone else is directly related to the openness and honesty we experience in our own relationships with God
If we don't allow God to comfort us, it is doubtful that we will know how to offer His comfort to others.

i. The caregiver will gain from the experience of comforting more than words can express
The privilege of loving others in their time of need puts "feet" on Paul's words: "Be imitators of God, therefore, as dearly loved children and live a life of love, just as Christ loved us and gave Himself up for us as a fragrant offering and sacrifice to God" (Eph. 5:1-2).

3. An overview of the training
While the training may not seem as specific or inclusive as you might like to ease the fear of something new, the concepts under-

127

stood and principles applied will make all the difference in our ability to reach out and offer comfort in love. People usually reach out with good intentions, and then quickly become absorbed by the various needs or the seeming impossibility of the situation. At such a time, only the strong survive.

Simply put, reaching out to others is best accomplished with a big heart and an honest understanding of both the struggles of this world and the true meaning of hope. Most of us have a difficult time reaching out due to fear and insecurity—not due to a lack of training or skill. Love, seasoned with truth, accomplishes much.

# FOURTEEN

## Details and Maintenance
## of the Program

Every program is only as good as its execution and maintenance. This chapter will deal with the details of keeping the program running smoothly and efficiently. Again, church size and the structure of the leadership will necessitate a fine-tuning of the program itself, but the following will serve to initiate the process.

**Matching Caregivers to Those Who Need Comforting**
Once people have been selected and trained for the job, a pairing of the volunteers with those who have a need is relatively simple. At this point, the church staff will have a basic idea of the personalities involved in the program, and the questionnaire will provide the information about who is comfortable in what circumstances.

My suggestion is to make a master list of volunteers, indicating the areas in which they feel free to minister, and their current availability. Also keep a master list of those in need. Then, as the church becomes aware of a need, the family or individual needing comfort can be directed to someone who wants to share in their pain. A few telephone calls should find a willing volunteer fairly quickly.

Someone on the pastoral staff can then visit or call the family or individual in need, sharing concern and letting the sufferer know that someone from the church wants to stay more closely in touch. From there, the program commences.

129

Some volunteers will want to work as a husband-wife team. Some young people or singles will also want to be involved. Particular notice should be made to inviting young people into the comfort-giving network. Assigning them to other young people who are having difficulty or to an elderly person who needs someone who cares can expose them to an important ministry within the church and to their own gifts.

### Sample 1
*Matching Caregivers to Those in Need*

| Name/ Address/ Phone of Caregiver | Expertise/ Interest | Dates of Last Assignment | Person/ Family | Date Assigned | Date Completed |
| --- | --- | --- | --- | --- | --- |
| Janet Jacob 2333 Diamond Cr. Dallas 214 444-4444 | illness, death, depression | 10/5/91– 11/5/92 | John Smith | 2/5/93 | |

### Sample 2
*Individuals/Families in Need*

| Name/Address/ Phone of Person or Family in Need | Specific Need | Date of Information | Assigned to Caregiver |
| --- | --- | --- | --- |
| John Smith 1221 Wren Way Dallas 214 333-3333 | depression John's wife died last month. | 2/3/93 | 2/5/93 J. Jacob |

Both forms, working together, can give the pastoral staff a picture of the needs of the church. If all requests are logged on the master list, then those in need can be assigned to a caregiver almost immediately.

While the forms may seem somewhat sterile or formal in

nature, they provide a visual picture of those involved in the program on both ends of the spectrum. They also help to ensure that no family or individual slips through the cracks, so to speak. At a glance, the pastoral staff can make certain that the needs of the people are being met and that those who are interested in serving are getting the opportunity.

The master list should be kept at church, accessible only to the pastoral staff.

## The Initial Visit and Assessment
People generally work best when there is a framework for the initial visit. Something as simple as a few questions to ask can start the relationship on a good note. Sample 3 gives a suggested format.

In the early days of the new relationship, it is most important to build comfort and trust and to evaluate the basic needs of the sufferer. It is my suggestion that caregivers keep notes on the family or individual assigned to them. They then can remember pertinent information and inform the pastoral staff of any special needs or of progress.

The summary need not be detailed, simply a few notes as a reminder. The object isn't to sterilize or formalize the relationship, but to facilitate the giving of comfort.

(Note: The caregiver should not read the questions and write the answers as if taking a survey. Keep the questions and answers in mind, and complete the information after leaving.)

Sample 3
*Initial Visit and Assessment*

Name:                                                     Phone:
Address:
Family Members:

What kind of suffering is this family/individual facing?

How much does the sufferer seem to understand about the problem?

Is the sufferer taking any medications?       If so, what kind?

What is the physician's name?

Family support available:

Group affiliations within the church:

Any physical needs of the family:

Spiritual and emotional climate of the family:

Special needs of the family/individual:

Other notes:

### Recording and Updating the Records
Most pastors prefer to keep the basic information in a file. This gives the pastoral staff the opportunity to brush up on the family before a visit. This also gives the pastoral staff a way to keep abreast of the situation. ALL RECORDS MUST BE KEPT CONFIDENTIAL.

One idea is for the caregiver to photocopy the initial questionnaire or any notes made, placing one copy in the confidential records of the church and retaining the other for personal use. Another idea is to keep the actual record at the church, retaining personal notes for future contact.

It is also imperative to update the records from time to time to indicate progress and special needs. Again, this gives the pastoral staff a chance to follow through on those individuals and families who continue to need support.

### A Network of Professionals
Most churches have members who have training in certain areas. For instance, there may be physicians or nurses in the church. There may also be professional counselors or social workers.

Check with those specialists. If they will permit, compile a list of names and numbers of those who can be called on to offer information to the caregivers. This will give those volunteers a sense of confidence and a place to turn if there is a problem that needs clarification or direction.

For instance, a caregiver may be assigned to someone with cancer or some other disease. That caregiver may want to learn a bit more about the disease itself. Likewise, someone may be assigned to a person on medication for depression. Talking with a psychologist in the church may help the caregiver understand more about the side effects and purposes of that medication.

Perhaps the person in pain wants to meet others who are experiencing the same struggle. The social workers may be aware of support networks or other groups located in your city that could help the hurting one. Maybe an elderly person who is afraid of the nursing-home environment might benefit from some basic information about retirement centers and how they operate.

The professionals will not be called on to actually take charge of the sufferer's situation. Their function is to provide possible information to support the caregivers.

## A Key to the Success of the Program
Many factors come together to make the program either a success or a failure, the key lies simply in the attitude of the pastoral staff. As anyone in any business is aware, the attitude of the company is set by the ones who operate that company. The Christian church and your congregation are no different.

Jesus firmly believed in the working together of His body of believers in this world. His belief filtered down among the disciples so that men like Peter and Paul stood firmly on the same commitment to the working together of the church.

If the pastoral staff is excited about people reaching out to others in the church, then the individual members will likely catch the vision and join in the privilege.

Certainly not all members will want to become personally involved. Some have so many time constraints already they will not be able to take on another commitment.

Many, however, will enjoy reaching out to fellow believers who are in need of comfort. Encourage your church to come together to build up, minister to, and reach out.

## Ongoing Training and Support for Volunteers
I have found that many caregivers like to go through the training program more than once. After they have had some experi-

ence in comforting, they feel that the information becomes more helpful.

Organizing social events can also keep the spirits high of those who are volunteering in the program. That way they are able to spend time with one another and enjoy the company.

Another helpful opportunity is to design several optional seminars throughout the year that focus attention on a specific area of caregiving. This way, those volunteers who are interested can learn more about that area of comforting others.

Professionals in the church and in the community will probably be honored to conduct such seminars or to inform the church, on a regular basis, of ongoing educational opportunities.

One final suggestion. Conduct a regular meeting at the church for the volunteers. On a monthly basis, for example, volunteers can meet with someone on the pastoral staff for support. These regular meetings work wonders! They keep the church staff and the caregivers united in a ministry of love.

## Appreciation and Opportunity

The main goals to keep in mind for the maintenance of the program are appreciation and opportunity.

*Appreciation.* No matter how pure the motives, everyone who is serving wants to be appreciated and sense that what they are doing is significant. This isn't about pride or selfish desires; it is simply about feeling appreciated for a job well done.

Most volunteers will say that the appreciation isn't necessary. They are sharing their services because they care; and, besides, the reward comes from the caring relationship itself.

Still, much is communicated through appreciation. In fact, the sense of doing something significant can provide energy, desire, and a great deal of motivation.

Take the time to appreciate those who are part of the ministry of care and concern.

*Opportunity.* When people attend training sessions, they are ready to get involved. Their selection, their desire, their training have all come together, and they want the opportunity to begin their service.

An important step to maintaining the program can be found in the opportunities afforded those who volunteer. Don't keep them waiting! They'll accept just about as much opportunity as you can dish out. If the burden becomes too heavy, they'll be right out on the front lines recruiting new volunteers.

Take care of the ones who step up to serve. They want to use their gifts to comfort God's people, and they deserve the chance.

# FIFTEEN

## The Ongoing Role
## of the Minister

The role of the minister is complex and full. Just as the head of the family gives shape to its members, so does the minister give shape to the church. The program will neither continue nor be successful if the minister is not involved with prayer, commitment, and blessing.

When Jesus left His disciples in this world, He left them with a solid system of support and encouragement in their work. The ongoing role of the pastor in the ministry of care and concern is like that ongoing presence of our Savior.

### "Not Bailing Out"
Put in modern language, one of the promises Jesus clearly made to His disciples was that He wasn't "bailing out." Though His work in this world was done, He would not leave them alone. His job hadn't ended. It had just changed scope.

The same analogy applies to the role of a minister in a program of care and concern. While one purpose for establishing a ministry of comfort is to support the church staff in their work, the motive of the minister is hardly one of "bailing out."

A ministry of care and concern established in the church is designed to support the role of the pastoral staff, not usurp that role. In a way, the volunteers serve as additional hands, feet, eyes, and ears for the ministers.

This program won't bring the pastor's role in comforting to an end. In fact, it probably won't even slow it down. What the program will do is allow for a more concentrated effort toward comforting those who are in pain.

## Unfolding the Truth

When Jesus left His disciples, He promised them the Spirit of Truth to be their guide. What a wonderful thought!

So many times I wonder if I'm doing the right thing, only to be reminded that the Spirit is there to guide me into truth. Sometimes I miss or avoid His leading, but that doesn't change the nature of God's provision.

One of the most significant ongoing roles of the minister lies in the teaching and reminding of truth. The more the congregation understands truth, the better their ability to live in this world honoring God and loving His people. The more the caregivers understand truth, the more valuable their offerings of comfort will be.

## Recounting the Lessons

No matter how thorough the training program, volunteers will only remember a portion of the material. Not only are we limited in what we can recall, but are limited by our experiences. Not until the volunteers are involved in caregiving will they begin to understand much of what was taught.

The pastoral staff can serve to remind the caregivers of the lessons they have learned in days and trainings gone by. Pastors generally have vast experience in "being there" through various painful times. Such experience on the part of the staff is invaluable to the volunteer caregivers, especially once they are in the business of offering comfort.

## Providing Resources

Who is more resourceful for the believer than the Spirit of God? How many times have you or I felt we had reached a dead end, only to discover God's creative ways?

There will be times when the caregivers feel completely dried up. Either the ones they are seeking to comfort take a turn for the worse, or the techniques seem to do little to offer support to the one in pain. Sometimes life itself becomes demanding, and the caregiver loses the personal sense of creativity or commitment.

137

The pastoral staff can do much in the way of offering resources. All the way from sharing personal stories to suggesting books or other materials—the pastoral staff can provide the much-needed resources to carry on.

### Encouraging Rest and Refreshment

Though members of the pastoral staff themselves may have a difficult time "taking a break," they can watch for signs of weariness among the caregivers and suggest a rest or a change of pace.

One of my favorite suggestions is really quite simple. Conduct some research and discover what programs are offered by local hospitals or service organizations. After the research is complete, suggest that the caregivers attend outside training sessions or conferences so they can explore new ways of comforting. In this manner they will acquaint themselves with others who are serving in similar ways. Sometimes, just getting a different view can offer refreshment.

Another favorite suggestion is also simple and a great deal of fun. Organize a get-together for those in the caregiving program. Around a meal or a time of fellowship, volunteers can support one another and offer fresh insights and ideas. Fun, laughter, singing, and sharing can produce great refreshment to weary souls.

### Bringing the Volunteers Together

Most of us do not look forward to adding one more meeting to our agendas, but this meeting will benefit both the attendees and the ministerial staff. Bring the caregivers together on a regular basis to share experiences and concerns with one another.

The names of those being cared for do not need to be part of the actual conversation, but a certain rapport will occur as the caregivers share their growth with one another. By suggesting possible comforts, generating new ideas, offering consolation, and just listening, a much-needed and highly valued network of mutual accomplishment and service will be born.

Not only will such meetings keep the volunteers in contact with one another, they also will keep the church staff in contact with a ministry that is very important.

## Modeling a Life of Service

Those who are involved in the caregiving program will come in close contact with the pastoral staff in the church. For the first time, some will even get to know those who are responsible for leading this body of believers.

All the words in the world cannot take the place of pastoral modeling. While the conversations, training sessions, and follow-up meetings will provide great insight, the best insight will come as the caregivers watch the pastoral staff serve one another and the community of believers.

How the minister relates to the rest of the staff, how the work is shared and supported, how the staff serves and listens to one another, how the believers in the church are supported and loved—all of these elements will add to the privilege of being part of the support network of the church. Much will be gained by the volunteers as they work more closely to broaden the role of the minister.

# SIXTEEN

## Support Groups and the Church

The ministry of caregiving is a layered ministry in the church. First, the pastor or pastoral staff want to be involved when church members are hurting. Second, laypeople who have offered their services of caregiving can broaden the ministry by supporting people through their difficult times.

Third, the use of support groups within the church can multiply the efforts of caregivers and introduce hurting people to others who've experienced similar pains. This latter layer of caregiving is usually the last to unfold because it involves careful planning and supervision. Only since the 1980s has this aspect of ministry in the church taken hold.

### The Purpose of Support Groups
The primary purpose of support groups is to bring together people who are suffering or have suffered a particular loss or pain. The idea is that in the presence of those who've experienced similar sufferings, people are more likely to gain perspective and work through the difficult times.

In a support group, that feeling of, "I'm the only one who's ever felt this way" or, "I wonder if anyone in the church can relate to me" is immediately replaced with a feeling of relief and identification. For years, churches have organized their Sunday School programs around this idea.

Young marrieds are often grouped together in the church. Singles generally share a class together. Widows and widowers

140

usually join together to offer support to one another. And children and adolescents certainly find their own peer support within the structure of the church. Evidently, the idea works beautifully!

The surface goal of support groups is to bring people together who share similar experiences or roles in life. The goal is a healthy way to offer support to people throughout life's passages.

## A Growing Range of Topics

Most churches have little trouble seeing the value of organizing Sunday School programs around similar life experiences, but many struggle with the more current use of share groups whose ministries range all the way from alcohol abuse to eating disorders.

Should the church itself be involved in the wider range of issues? It is my belief that we must. Can't those members who suffer from some of these difficulties find help outside the church? Certainly. But do we want people in the church to be ashamed to admit their needs, or do we want to be part of their solution?

Taking a look at issues that involve a greater number of people in the church, we find a need to educate our members about these issues and help people who struggle with these stresses find the support that they need. Let's review the possibilities of pains and circumstances that are best endured in the company of others.

*Possible Support Groups in the Church*
- Eating Disorders: bulimia and anorexia nervosa
- Alcohol Abuse: both individual and family concerns
- Gambling
- Obsessive Disorders
- Sexual Addiction
- Divorce
- Single Parents
- People who struggle with cancer, multiple sclerosis, Alzheimer's disease, Parkinson's disease, diabetes, lupus, and a myriad of other physical illnesses and constraints
- Adult Children of Alcoholics
- Victims of Sexual Abuse

- Sexual Abusers
- Incest
- Child Victims of Physical Abuse
- Parent Offenders of Physical Abuse
- Physical Abuse within a Marriage
- Workaholism
- Stress
- Caring for Aging Parents
- Caring for Dependent Children
- Victims of AIDS
- Children with AIDS
- Unemployment or Underemployment
- Widows and Widowers
- Chronic Pain
- Women in the Workplace

The list goes on.

It is not my intent to suggest that churches should not make good use of programs and support groups widely established in the community. It is, however, my belief that the local church should take part in the overall ministry to its members, providing support groups or at the very least inviting support groups to take place within the walls of the church.

## Educating the Leadership and the People

Nothing can be done to provide a healthy network of support until those who are leaders in the church make themselves aware of the needs and of the programs that have been established to help meet those needs. To borrow a worn-out argument, it seems that the church is often the last one to know about these things.

I first suggest a little work on the part of the church staff. There are a number of books on the market (see Appendix B) and a number of good community efforts that can serve to initiate the education process. The staff should acquaint themselves with the various struggles people are facing, not to become experts in every field, but to become aware of the stressful situations that the members of the congregation might face.

Next, make a list of books on the various topics, and even have them available in the church library, if possible. This way, people who are experiencing various needs can at least research the issue on their own. Meanwhile, others in the church interested in expanding their understanding of these issues will have a suggested starting place. Being pointed in a direction certainly begins the process of communication or healing.

I also suggest having one-day "update" seminars where various needs and helpful materials can be discussed. Ministers, volunteers involved in the caregiving program, and church members at large will find the seminars quite helpful for providing both information and understanding.

### Removing the Mystique

Perhaps the greatest gift that information gives is simply the gift of removing the mystique that surrounds certain issues of pain. I don't think I would be presumptuous, for example, in saying that most church members do not understand AIDS, eating disorders, or alcoholism and its effects. In fact, most are afraid of these sufferings. Therefore, their reality remains shrouded in mystique.

If the pastoral staff models concern and a desire to be educated in these areas, then the members of the congregation will want to become aware. I'm certainly not promising that all members will approve of or like the addition of support groups in many of these areas, but I am suggesting that as the leadership models concern, needs will surface in the church.

### Tailor-Making Your Program

To easily explain, I have divided support groups into two areas. Most of today's concerns can fall under these two "umbrellas," and seeing the need visually aids in our understanding.

Most pastors function best when they can visualize the structure of support groups and when they can organize those groups that begin within the walls of the church. Perhaps the following lists will provide a framework from which to begin:

| *Support Groups for Emotional and Physical Needs or Losses* | *Support Groups for Addictive Behaviors and Their Victims* |
|---|---|
| Cancer support groups | Alcoholics Anonymous |

Widows and widowers
Grief support groups
Parents who've lost
  children
Children who care for
  aging adults
Parents of children with
  special needs
Children who've lost
  parents
Single parent families
Singles
Aging adults
Support for chronic pain
Support for chronic illnesses
Spouses of the critically
  or chronically ill
Unwed mothers
Support for the unemployed
Support for divorced adults
Support for children of
  divorce

Adult children of alcoholics
Spouses of alcoholics
Drug addictions
Eating disorders
Sexual addictions
Compulsive behaviors
Victims of sexual abuse
Victims of physical abuse
Sexual offenders
Parents who abuse
Young children of alcoholics
Spouses who abuse
Workaholism
Victims of emotional abuse
Gamblers anonymous
Spenders anonymous

I have been as creative as I can be to provide a list of many possible networks of support. There are many needs in today's society and support groups offer a healthy way of working through those needs and halting their proliferation.

Do we have more problems in today's world? Perhaps. But I think if you'll examine the list, you'll find that most of the problems are not new.

What we seem to have is fewer ways to hide the problems. And I, for one, am thankful for the disclosure. We have invited people to open up, and they are simply presenting pains that have been held in or repeated for years.

### Taking It Slowly
The solution to the problem of so many needs lies in taking the ministry of comfort one step at a time, one day at a time. We don't have to provide all of the groups right now; we have only to begin to care.

Start with the caregivers—those volunteers who want to be part of the ministry of offering comfort. The support groups will naturally flow from that ministry of comfort. By then, lay leaders will arise to lend their time and interest.

When we look to a list of so many needs, we tend to give up before we begin. Don't look to what you aren't yet providing. Look to what you can begin to provide through a few concerned caregivers. The rest of the ministry will find its place as the loving abounds.

## Leadership

Most churches that boast of successful support groups have trained the leaders from within. It takes some additional training to take on that responsibility, but it does not take a professional counselor or physician. Though there are some who would argue with me on this point, by and large the most proven support groups are led from the inside out.

At first, the leadership will come from trained caregivers, willing to take on an additional aspect to their ministry. After awhile, the leadership can be turned over to a member of the group who is still in process yet well along the road to growth and recovery.

Does the lay leader then step out of the ministry? No. The lay leader simply steps back and allows those who've experienced the pain to walk with others through the suffering.

The lay leader can offer support, insights from God's Word, answers to a few questions here and there; but the primary purpose of the support group isn't one of instruction. The purpose is sharing.

Let me add one word of encouragement. If the pastoral staff feels inadequate to facilitate support groups or uneasy about available leaders, remember that there's a world of social services out there, amply equipped and probably quite eager to help you establish and maintain such a ministry within the church.

## Purpose, Format, and Follow-Through

The purpose of support groups lies in the relationships established within the groups themselves. Take a support group for widowers, for example. New members will be added all the time who are freshly confronted with the loss of their spouses and the pain of such loss. Those who are farther down the line in the healing process are there to offer comfort and a listening ear.

Since friendships are built on the stability of the share group, members require honesty and vulnerability. After all, how do you bring ten widowers together without openness and transparency? They understand a bit of what it means to walk in one another's shoes.

The format of a share group is really very simple. For the most part, sharing is the foundation of what happens during the hour or two in which the group meets.

It is best to have a moderator who organizes and gives shape to the meeting, but that moderator is not a teacher. Teaching is done by all the members of the group.

Each group is organized differently because each will have its own particular flavor. Some like to begin with a topic agreed upon before the meeting. Some like to leave the agenda completely open. Some like to require everyone to form a circle to participate in some way. Some make participation strictly a choice of each member of the group.

Some have a fairly strict attendance requirement in order to keep as much integrity and direction as possible. Some don't mind who comes or how often.

Some support groups ask new members to share their stories. Some rotate stories each week, updating their growth and needs.

Whatever the format, the point is that support groups are rarely organized around strict timetables or set topics. Most simply want to provide an atmosphere of love and acceptance.

Perhaps the most important point in talking about follow-through is this: When someone reaches out with today's pain to say "I need help and friends," we don't want to lose that person to tomorrow's depression. It is best to select a member of the support group to serve as the "welcoming committee" to new faces.

A new member may not be active in church. He may need some individual help or she may need medical care or counseling. The following-through on members of the group is an important function of support.

### The Importance of Size
Even though a Sunday School class of senior adults represents a grouping of people with similar needs and circumstances in life,

such a class does not usually qualify as a support group.

Why? Because more than ten people is too many to be adequately known, heard, and understood. When we are one in a very large number, we rarely speak from our hurt or ask for help. A support group needs to be small enough to provide intimacy.

I suggest no more than eight to ten members, simply because that number of people almost ensures that everyone who wants to participate can. It is a manageable size for discussion, interaction, prayer, and comfort.

What if the group begins to gain popularity? Simple enough; divide the group into two groups and continue to add smaller networks as people seek support.

One very popular format goes something like this: Have all the support groups that deal with physical or emotional needs and losses meet on a certain night of the week.

As the meeting begins, start with singing as a group and praying for one another. Introduce visitors and make announcements that have to do with everyone.

Then, divide into the smaller groups for the remainder of the evening. This enables everyone to spend some time together. It also provides an easy way to organize new groups as the need arises.

When a person has been part of a group for some time and has grown in his or her insights and personal life, invite that person to become the nucleus for one of the new groups that is starting. As you can see, this will broaden the ministry, allow the church to retain some measure of control over the situation, and use the gifts of growing members who are experiencing healing in their pain.

## Concerns about Support Groups

*Becoming "Comfortable."* One of my concerns has always been the need to integrate people of various experiences, but most professionals agree that identification with people in similar circumstances needs to precede the integration. What I am saying is this: I am always concerned that those who are suffering step out of the victim role and into the responsible role when the time is right.

Using members of the group to facilitate additional groups aids in this concern, as does inviting the members of the group to share their growths with the wider church body.

We tend to label people, and people tend to grow comfortable in their labels. We need to help those who are hurting walk on to new possibilities of leadership and service.

*A Glass Wall.* Another concern I have is that the success of support groups (something we pray for!) can also create a minichurch effect. So content are people to remain in contact with others who understand their circumstances that they tend to find a haven there and not reach back into the larger church community.

The flip side of the coin is also a factor. To those people in the church at large who do not understand all of these support groups, the less contact they have, the better. If we're not careful, a "glass wall" develops, almost creating two churches within the congregation.

We need to integrate the support network with the larger network within the church. People who don't understand need to learn to communicate with those who struggle. And those who struggle need to step out of the "they don't understand" mold and into the realization that they need to play a vital role in the church.

Church leadership can greatly facilitate the integration, as can encouraged communication between all members of the body.

Remember, those who act indifferent are usually afraid of what they don't understand. And those who act reluctant to play a part are usually afraid of rejection.

The purpose of the support group ministry is to aid people who are suffering in their progress through life. We don't want to create an oasis where there is no more need for growth. Neither do we want, any longer, to pretend that the sufferers don't exist.

Support groups can have a tremendous impact on the congregation—and on the lives of those in need of comfort.

# SECTION FIVE:
## A Storehouse of Information

Therefore encourage one another and build each other up, just as in fact you are doing.

1 Thessalonians 5:11

# APPENDIX A:
## Supportive Ministries in the Community at Large

The following is a partial list of resources that are available to the local church as well as to the individual in need. All of these organizations play a vital role in the community, and most would be willing to lend support to the ministry of comfort within the church.

There will be local chapters of many of these organizations in your town. Simply call and let them know what you are doing and what you need. I am certain they'll be more than happy to work with the local church in providing help to the hurting and the caregivers alike!

Too often Christians are "suspicious" of secular organizations, but most of those organizations are staffed by Christians and non-Christians alike, eager to serve and well aware of the needs of people in this world.

As much as is possible, work with the organizations in your community. A working relationship can only better the help that is available to those in need.

### Major National and International Help Organizations

American Cancer Society
Mental Health and Mental Retardation
The American Red Cross
The Peace Corps
United Way
The Salvation Army

### Organizations That Generally Operate through Local Chapters

Hospice
Ronald McDonald House

Alcoholics Anonymous, Al-Anon, ACA, and Al a Teen
Alcoholics Anonymous is the group for those who struggle with alcohol addiction. Al-Anon is for the spouses of those who struggle with alcohol addiction. ACA (Adult Children of Alcoholics) is for adults who come face-to-face with the addictions of their parents. And Al a Teen is for teenagers living with an alcoholic parent.

**Emotional, Physical, and Mental Health Services***

| | |
|---|---|
| ADA (Diabetes Information Service) | 800 232-3472 |
| AIDS Hotline | 800 342-AIDS |
| in Spanish | 800 342-SIDA |
| National AIDS Information Clearinghouse | 800 458-5231 |
| AIDS Helpline (drug abusers) | 800 662-HELP |
| ALS Association | 800 782-4747 |
| Al-Anon Family Group Headquarters | 800 356-9996 |
| Alcohol and Drug Addiction Treatment Center | 800 382-4357 |
| Alcoholics Anonymous World Services | 212 686-1100 |
| Alzheimer's and Related Disorders | 800 272-3900 |
| American Cancer Society | 800 227-2345 |
| American Mental Health Fund | 800 433-5959 |
| American Paralysis Association | 800 225-0292 |
| American Red Cross | 800 238-6393 |
| American Trauma Society | 800 556-7890 |
| Battering and Rape Alliance | 800 356-2369 |
| Bulimia/Anorexia Self-Help | 800 227-4785 |
| Bulimia/Anorexia Self-Help Crisis Line | 800 762-3334 |
| Cancer Information Hotline | 800 525-3777 |
| Cancer Information Service | 800 4-CANCER |
| Child Abuse Hotline | 800 4-A-CHILD |
| Children's Hospice International | 800 24-CHILD |
| Children's Wish Foundation International | 800 323-9474 |
| Cocaine Hotline | 800 COC-AINE |
| Covenant House (runaway children) | 800 999-9999 |
| Cottage Program (alcohol) | 800 752-6100 |
| Diabetes Information Service | 800 627-6872 |
| Drug Abuse Resistance Education Program | 800 223-DARE |
| in Spanish | 800 66-AYUDA |
| Epilepsy Foundation | 800 EFA-1000 |
| Hospice Link | 800 331-1620 |
| Huntington's Disease (general information line) | 800 345-4372 |
| Just Say No Kids Club | 800 258-2766 |

*Phone numbers current as of January 1992.

| | |
|---|---|
| Lupus Research Institute | 800 82-LUPUS |
| Medic-Alert Foundation International | 800 ID-ALERT |
| Mental Health and Mental Retardation | 800 252-8154 |
| National Association for Domestic Violence | 800 333-SAFE |
| National Association of Rehabilitation Facilities | 800 368-3513 |
| National Association of Sickle Cell Disease | 800 421-8453 |
| National Association of Working Women | 800 522-0925 |
| National Center for Missing and Exploited Children | 800 843-5678 |
| National Chaplin's Association | 800 486-9436 |
| National Criminal Justice Referral system (victims) | 800 851-3420 |
| Victims Resource Center | 800 627-6872 |
| National Council on Alcoholism and Drug Dependency | 800 475-HOPE |
| National Council on Child Abuse and Family Violence | 800 222-2000 |
| National Foundation for Depressive Illness | 800 248-4344 |
| National Hotline for Domestic Violence | 800 333-SAFE |
| National Information Center for Children with Handicaps | 800 999-5599 |
| National Information Center for Orphan Drugs and Rare Diseases | 800 336-4797 |
| National Information System for Health Related Services (disabled/chronically ill under 21) | 800 922-9234 |
| National Institute on Drug Abuse | 800 662-HELP |
| National Reye's Syndrome Foundation | 800 233-7393 |
| | 800 221-SIDS |
| National Ranaway Switchboard (also suicide) | 800 621-4000 |
| | 800 231-6946 |
| National Sexual Addiction Hotline | 800 321-2066 |
| Order of United Commercial Travelers of America (retarded children) | 800 848-0123 |
| Hospital referral line | 800 237-5055 |
| Parents Anonymous (stressed parents) | 800 421-0353 |
| The Salvation Army | 800 292-7058 |
| Sexual Addiction Information | 800 321-2273 |
| Sudden Infant Death Syndrome (SIDS) Alliance | 800 638-SIDS |
| | 800 221-SIDS |
| The Peace Corps | 800 424-8580 |
| United Way | 800 833-5948 |

153

| | |
|---|---|
| Veterans of the Vietnam War | 800 VIET-NAM |
| Vietnam Veterans of America | 800 424-7275 |
| "Why Me" National Organization for Support (Breast Cancer Support) | 800 221-2141 |

**Additional organizations for specialized support:**

**For sexual addictions:**
>Pure Life Ministries
>P.O. Box 345
>Crittendon, KY 41030
>Helpline: 800-635-1866

**For codependency issues:**
>Mellody Enterprises
>P.O. Box 1739
>Wickenburg, AZ 85358
>Helpline: (602) 684-5075

**For homosexual issues:**
>Exodus International
>P.O. Box 3232
>San Rafael, CA 94912

>Love in Action
>P.O. Box 2655
>San Rafael, CA 94912
>Helpline: (415) 454-0960

**For lay counseling and support group help:**
>CSC Ministries
>6255 West Northwest Hwy. Suite 320
>Dallas, TX 75225
>Helpline: (214) 363-6295

# APPENDIX B:
## Books and Other Resources

There are a number of helpful books on the market, each designed with a particular need in mind. While a book cannot address every facet of pain or healing in a given situation, it can prove invaluable for the hurting one and for the caregiver. Please accept the following suggestions as a place to begin.

### Concerning Abortion

*Abortion: a Rational Look at an Emotional Issue*, R.C. Sproul, NavPress

### Concerning Abuse and Personal Pain

*Counseling for Family Violence and Abuse*, Grant L. Martin, Word
*Healing for Adult Children of Alcoholics*, Sara Martin, Broadman
*Healing for Damaged Emotions*, David Seamands, Victor Books
*Healing of Memories*, David Seamands, Victor Books
*Healing Victims of Sexual Abuse*, Paul Sandford, Victory House
*Pain and Pretending*, Rich Buhler, Thomas Nelson Publishers
*The Courage to Heal Workbook: For Women and Men Survivors of Child Sexual Abuse*, Laura Davis, Harper & Row

### Concerning Addictions

*Addicted to Love*, Steve Arterburn, Vine Books/Servant Publications
*Addiction and Grace*, May Ger, Harper & Row
*Adult Children: Legal/Emotional Divorce*, Jim Conway, InterVarsity Press
*Alcoholism: A Family Matter*, Edited, Health Communications

*Anorexia Nervosa and Bulimia: A Handbook for Counselors and Therapists*, Patricia Neuman and Patricia Halvorson, Van Noss Reinhold

*Breaking the Cycle of Addiction*, Patricia O'Gorman and Philip Oliver Diaz, Health Communications

*Children of Alcoholics*, Robert Ackerman, Fireside

*Counseling for Problems of Self-Control*, Richard Walters, Word

*Counseling for Substance Abuse and Addiction*, Steven Van Cleave, Walter Byrd, and Kathy Revell, Word

*Counseling Those with Eating Disorders*, Raymond Vath, Word

*Drug Addictions: Learn About It Before Your Kids Do*, Pierre Andre, Health Communications

*Facing Shame: Families in Recovery*, Merle A. Fossum and Marilyn J. Mason, Norton

*Games Alcoholics Play*, Claude M. Steiner, Ballantine

*Games People Play*, Eric Berne, Ballantine

*Habitation of Dragons*, Keith Miller, Word

*Healing for Adult Children of Alcoholics*, Sara Martin, Broadman

*Healing Life's Hidden Addictions*, Dr. Archibald Hart, Servant Publications

*Imperative People*, Dr. Les Carter, Thomas Nelson Publishers

*Out of the Shadows: Understanding Sexual Addiction*, Patrick Carnes, CompCare

*Pain and Pretending*, Rich Buhler, Thomas Nelson Publishers

*Recovery from Co-dependency*, Laura Weiss and Jonathan B. Weiss, Health Communications

*Surviving Addiction: A Guide for Alcoholics, Drug Addicts, and Their Families*, Dennis Daley, Gardner Press

*Surviving an Eating Disorder: Strategies for Families and Friends*, Michele Siegel, Harper & Row

*The Courage to Go On: Life After Addiction*, Cynthia Rowland McClure, Baker Books

*The Peter Pan Syndrome*, Dan Kiley, Dodd & Mead

*The Road Less Travelled*, M. Scott Peck, Simon and Schuster

*We Are Driven: The Compulsive Behaviors America Applauds*, Dr. Robert Helmfelt, Dr. Frank Minirth & Dr. Paul Meier, Thomas Nelson Publishers

*When I Say No I Feel Guilty*, Manuel J. Smith, Bantam

**Concerning Adolescence**

*Coping with Teenage Depression*, Kathleen McCoy, New American Library

*Teenagers Talk about Suicide*, Marion Crook, New York Press

*Teens Talk about Alcohol/Alcoholism*, Paul Dolmetsch and Gail Mauriette, Doubleday

## Concerning Children

*Dibs in Search of Self*, Virginia Axline, Ballantine Books
*Families of Handicapped Children*, Marion Duckworth, David C. Cook
*Kids Who Carry Our Pain*, Dr. Robert Hemfelt & Dr. Paul Warren, Thomas Nelson Publishers
*Sometimes God Has a Kids's Face*, Bruce Ritter, Covenant House
*The Hurried Child*, David Elkind, Addison-Wesley Publishing Company

## Concerning Codependency

*Adult Children: Legal/Emotional Divorce*, Jim Conway, InterVarsity Press
*Beyond Codependency*, Melody Beattie, Harper & Row
*Codependency and Me*, edited, Health Communications
*Codependent No More*, Melody Beattie, Hazelden
*Facing Codependence*, Pia Mellody, Harper Collins Publishers
*Healing the Shame that Binds You*, John Bradshaw, Health Communications
*Homecoming*, John Bradshaw, Bantam Books
*One-Way Relationships*, Alfred Ells, Thomas Nelson Publishers
*Overcoming Codependency*, Pat Springle, Word
*Pain and Pretending*, Rich Buhler, Thomas Nelson Publishers
*The Language of Letting Go*, Melody Beattie, Harper & Row

## Concerning Emotions

*Healing for Damaged Emotions*, David Seamands, Victor Books
*Healing the Angry Heart*, Keith Miller, Aglow Publications
*Living Beyond Our Fears*, Bruce Larson, Harper & Row
*Managing Your Emotions*, Erwin Lutzer, Victor Books
*The Gift of Feeling*, Paul Tournier, John Knox Press
*Uncovering Your Fears*, Norm Wright, Tyndale

## Concerning the Family

*Bradshaw on the Family*, John Bradshaw, Health Communications
*Family Secrets*, Rachel V., Harper & Row
*Mothers and Daughters*, Marie Chapian, Bethany House
*Shaking the Family Tree*, Dr. William Berman, Dr. Dale R. Doty, Jean Huff Graham, Victor Books

*The Secrets of the Family Tree*, Dave Carder, Dr. Earl Henslin, Dr. John Townsend, Dr. Henry Clark, Alice Brawand, Moody Press

## Concerning Grace and Forgiveness

*A Forgiving God in an Unforgiving World*, Ron Lee Davis, Harvest House Publishers
*Counseling and Guilt*, Earl Wislon, Word
*Forgive and Love Again*, John Nieder, Harvest House Publishers
*Forgiving Our Parents, Forgiving Ourselves*, Dr. David Stoop, Vine Books
*Freedom from the Performance Trap*, David Seamands, Victor Books
*Making Peace with Your Past*, Norm Wright, Fleming H. Revell

## Concerning Grief and Depression

*A Grief Observed*, C.S. Lewis, Harper & Row
*Comforting Those Who Grieve*, Doug Manning, Harper & Row
*Counseling the Depressed*, Archibald Hart, Word
*Courage to Grieve*, Judy Tatelbaum, Harper & Row
*Depression: Finding Hope and Meaning in Life's Darkest Shadow*, Don Baker & Emery Nester, Multnomah
*Grief*, Haddon Robinson, Zondervan
*Letter of Consolation*, Henri Nouwen, Harper & Row
*Loneliness*, Elisabeth Elliot, Oliver Nelson Publishers
*On Asking God Why*, Elisabeth Elliot, Fleming H. Revell Co.
*Path through Suffering*, Elisabeth Elliot, Servant Publications
*Rebuilding Your Broken World*, Gordon MacDonald, Thomas Nelson Publishers
*Recovering from the Loss of a Child*, Katherine Donnely, Dodd
*Recovering from the Loss of a Sibling*, Katherine Donnely, Dodd
*Seasons of Grief*, Donna Gaffney, New American Library, Inc.
*Too Early Frost*, Gerald Oosterveen, Zondervan
*What Works When Life Doesn't*, Stuart Briscoe, Victor Books

## Concerning Homosexuality

*Beyond Rejection: The Church, Homosexuality, and Hope*, Don Baker, Multnomah
*Coming to Grips with Homosexuality*, Erwin Lutzer, Moody Press
*Counseling and Homosexuality*, Earl Wilson, Word
*Counseling the Homsexual*, Saia Mi, Bethany House

## Concerning Mercy

*Close Enough to Care*, Pat Springle, Word

*Comforting Those Who Grieve*, Doug Manning, Harper & Row
*Helping the Hurting*, Phillip Yancey, Multnomah
*Within the Shadow*, Shelley Chapin, Victor Books

## Concerning Parenting

*Building Your Child's Self Esteem*, Gary Smalley & John Trent, NavPress
*Dare to Discipline*, James Dobson, Tyndale House Publishers
*High Risk Children without a Conscience*, Ken Magid, Bantam Books
*Learning to Let Go*, Carol Kuykendal, Zondervan
*Parents and Children*, Jay Kesler, Victor Books
*Parents and Teenagers*, Jay Kesler, Victor Books
*Recovering from the Loss of a Child*, Katherine Donnely, Dodd
*Recovering from the Loss of a Sibling*, Katherine Donnely, Dodd
*Successful Single Parenting*, Gary Richmond, Harvest House Publishers
*Ten Mistakes Parents Make with Teenagers*, Jay Kesler, Wolgemuth & Hyatt

## Concerning Personal Growth

*A Long Obedience in the Same Direction*, Eugene Peterson, InterVarsity Press
*At the Breaking Point*, Jim Long, Campus Life Books
*Balancing Life's Demands*, J. Grant Howard, Multnomah
*Being Holy, Being Human*, Jay Kesler, Word
*Choices*, Lewis Smedes, Harper & Row
*Counseling and Self-Esteem*, David E. Carlson, Word
*Counseling and the Search for Meaning*, Paul Welter, Word
*Eating Problems for Breakfast*, Tim Hansel, Word
*Fearfully and Wonderfully Made*, Paul Brand and Phillip Yancey, Zondervan
*Finding Your Way Home*, Kenneth A. Schmidt, Regal Books
*Forgiving Our Parents, Forgiving Ourselves*, Dr. David Stoop, Vine Books
*Growing Strong in the Seasons of Life*, Chuck Swindoll, Multnomah
*Growing Deep in Christian Life*, Chuck Swindoll, Multnomah
*Holy Sweat* Tim Hansel, Word
*Homecoming*, John Bradshaw, Bantam Books
*Hunger for Healing*, Keith Miller, Harper & Row
*Inside Out*, Larry Crabb, NavPress
*Overcoming the Grasshopper Complex*, Erwin Lutzer, Victor Books
*Putting Away Childish Things*, David Seamands, Victor Books

*Putting Your Past Behind You*, Erwin Lutzer, Here's Life Publishers
*Restoring Your Spiritual Passion*, Gordon MacDonald, Thomas Nelson
   Publishers
*Run with the Horses*, Eugene Peterson, InterVarsity Press
*Stranger to Myself No More*, Karen Mains, Word
*The Art of Learning to Love Yourself*, Cecil Osborne, Zondervan
   Books
*The Art of Understanding Yourself*, Cecil Osborne, Zondervan Books
*The Peter Pan Syndrome*, Dan Kiley, Dodd and Mead
*The Road Less Travelled*, M. Scott Peck, Simon and Schuster
*The Search for Significance*, Robert S. McGee, Rapha Publishing
*Unfinished Business*, Donald Joy, Victor Books
*When I Relax I Feel Guilty*, Tim Hansel, David C. Cook Publishers

## Concerning Personal Testimony

*Joni*, Joni Eareckson Tada, Zondervan
*Joni: A Step Further*, Joni Eareckson Tada, Zondervan
*Lifelines*, Edith Schaeffer, Good News Publishers
*Within the Shadow*, Shelley Chapin, Victor Books
*You've Gotta Keep Dancing*, Tim Hansel, Word

## Concerning Physical and Emotional Suffering and Loss

*Affliction*, Edith Schaeffer, Fleming H. Revell Co.
*AIDS: The Ultimate Challenge*, Elisabeth Kubler-Ross, MacMillan
   Publishers
*Counseling in Times of Crisis*, Judson Swihart & Gerald Richardson,
   Word
*Courage to Begin Again*, Ron Lee Davis, Harvest House Publishers
*Dealing with Suicide*, John Throop, David C. Cook Publishers
*Death: The Final Stage of Growth*, Elisabeth Kubler-Ross, Simon and
   Schuster
*Disappointment with God*, Phillip Yancey, Zondervan
*Families of Handicapped Children*, Marion Duckworth, David C.
   Cook
*Hospice and Ministry*, Paul Irion, Abingdon
*My Journey Into Alzheimer's Disease*, Ron Lee Davis, Tyndale
*On Children and Death*, Elisabeth Kubler-Ross, MacMillan Publishers
*On Death and Dying*, Elisabeth Kubler-Ross, MacMillan Publishers
*Recovering from the Losses of Life*, Norm Wright, Fleming H. Revell
*Sudden Infant Death Syndrome*, Jan Culbertson, Johns Hopkins
*Surprised by Suffering*, R.C. Sproul, Tyndale House Publishers
*Waiting*, Ben Patterson, InterVarsity Press

*Where Is God When It Hurts?* Phillip Yancey, Zondervan
*Within the Shadow,* Shelley Chapin, Victor Books
*You've Gotta Keep Dancing,* Tim Hansel, Word

### Concerning Relationships

*Bonding: Relationships in the Image of God,* Donald Joy, Word
*Caring and Commitment,* Lewis Smedes, Harper & Row
*Caring Enough to Confront,* David Augsberger, Regal Books
*Caring Enough to Forgive,* David Augsberger, Regal Books
*Caring Enough to Hear and Be Heard,* David Augsberger, Regal Books
*Coming to Grips with Marital Conflict,* Erwin Lutzer, Moody Press
*Encouragement: Key to Caring,* Larry Crabb, Zondervan
*Forgivensss,* Charles Stanley, Thomas Nelson Publishers
*Freedom of Forgivensss,* David Augsberger, Moody Press
*Love, Acceptance, and Forgiveness,* Jerry Cook & Stanley Baldwin, Regal Books
*Love — No Strings Attached,* Rich Buhler, Thomas Nelson Publishers
*Making Real Friends in a Phony World,* Jim Conway, Zondervan
*Mothers and Daughters,* Marie Chapian, Bethany House
*New Choices New Boundaries,* Rich Buhler, Thomas Nelson Publishers
*One-Way Relationships,* Alfred Ells, Thomas Nelson Publishers
*Pain and Pretending,* Rich Buhler, Thomas Nelson Publishers
*Pulling Together when You're Pulled Apart,* Stuart and Jill Briscoe, Victor Books
*Say It with Love,* Howard Hendricks, Victor Books
*Seasons of a Marriage,* Norm Wright, Regal Books
*Sustaining Love, Healing Growth,* David Augsberger, Regal Books Publishers
*The Language of Love,* Gary Smalley & John Trent, Focus on the Family Publishing
*Trauma of Transparency,* J. Grant Howard, Multnomah
*Understanding People,* Larry Crabb, Zondervan

### Concerning Suicide

*Suicide, Why?* Adina Wrobleski, Afterwords
*Teenagers Talk about Suicide,* Marion Crook, NC Press

### Other Resources
There are numerous resources available to the church and to the individual. Video tapes and cassette tapes are often helpful for understanding pain and comfort at another level. While I could list a num-

ber of videotapes and cassette tape series that have been helfpul to me, I think it is best to suggest that the church develop a library of such materials. This way, every member of the church has access to help, and the pastoral staff can keep abreast of new ideas and insights.